Stefan Ramel is a leading barrister specialising in commercial and insolvency work. He is top-ranked in both Chambers and Partners and the Legal 500 for his insolvency work. He has appeared in numerous reported insolvency cases, including in relation to contested bankruptcy petitions. He is on the Attorney-General's Civil Panel of Counsel (A Panel; Regional) and sits part-time as a Recorder on the Western Circuit.

Govinder Chambay is a specialist insolvency practitioner who undertakes litigation and advisory work in all aspects of corporate and personal insolvency law. He was called to the bar in 2018 and is developing a substantial insolvency practice. Govinder has been recognised as a rising star in the 2025 and 2026 Legal 500 and as 'Up and Coming' in Chambers and Partners 2026. Alongside his wide-ranging insolvency practice, he has appeared in numerous cases concerning bankruptcy petitions acting for both creditors and debtors.

A Practical Guide to Contested Bankruptcy Petitions

A Practical Guide to Contested Bankruptcy Petitions

Stefan Ramel
Govinder Chambay

Law Brief Publishing

Published 2026 by Law Brief Publishing, an imprint of Law Brief Publishing Ltd
30 The Parks
Minehead
Somerset
TA24 8BT

www.lawbriefpublishing.com

Paperback: 978-1-918241-17-4

PREFACE

Bankruptcies are on the rise, at least according to the latest statistics by the Insolvency Service.[1] In our view, this is unsurprising - the last few years have been economically challenging, as perhaps best shown by the cost-of-living crisis.

Bankruptcy law is also currently very topical in the courts. For example, last year, the Court of Appeal had to resolve a fundamental question of whether an unregistered foreign judgment debt was capable of forming the basis of a bankruptcy petition.

We have no doubt in saying that being faced with a bankruptcy petition will rank amongst one of the most stressful experiences a person can be unfortunate enough to encounter. For creditors, it can be disheartening and often frustrating. It can also be, to the uninitiated, something of a minefield for lawyers, owing to the wealth of jurisprudence and procedural rules which need to be followed. Bankruptcy proceedings also proceed at a much quicker pace than a normal civil claim; time is of the essence, parties must act promptly to avoid losing the opportunity of raising and taking substantive and technical points.

Unsurprisingly, petitions are often defended with real vigour. Typically, a whole host of different points are taken, ranging from matters of principle to questions of whether procedure has been followed. The state of play also tends to change quite rapidly; it is not uncommon for evidence to be adduced at the last minute or indeed for very obscure points to be taken. The stakes are very high, after all.

The principles and procedures in relation to contested bankruptcy petitions are scattered amongst numerous decisions of the courts and in

---

1 https://www.gov.uk/government/statistics/individual-insolvencies-january-2026/commentary-individual-insolvency-statistics-january-2026#main-messages-for-england-and-wales

various fine textbooks on personal insolvency. But, there are no books, as far as we are aware, which deal exclusively and in one place with contested bankruptcy petitions. We have sought to fill this gap, in the hope that it will assist practitioners who are charged with dealing with such matters.

In this regard, there are practical matters in respect of contested bankruptcy petitions which are not usually dealt with in academic texts. We have aimed in this book to approach matters from not only a doctrinal academic perspective, but also through the lens of our joint practical experience of appearing in many bankruptcy petition cases.

To that end, this book explores heavyweight matters relating to jurisdiction right the way through to more technical matters such as procedure. An entire chapter is devoted to procedure which traces the evolution of a petition's existence all the way from the statutory demand to the petition's presentation and then hearing.

Our chapter on technical points covers the more common technical issues which can arise and the court's approach to them.

Equally, in chapter 4 we set out the numerous different types of ways that a petition may be contested. In that regard we drill down into practical concerns, including for instance, the type, quality and cogency of evidence required and the court's approach to applications to adjourn etc. We also explore more specialist matters such as insolvent administration orders and incapacity.

Again, much of our analysis is also interspersed with insights based on our own experience which is not often the subject of much (if any) consideration in the textbooks which we are aware of.

We hope that this book will provide useful and practical assistance to lawyers and insolvency practitioners alike as they navigate through this particular aspect of insolvency law.

We have endeavoured to state the law and procedural rules in force as at 31st December 2025.

Stefan Ramel
Govinder Chambay
January 2026

CONTENTS

CHAPTER ONE

INTRODUCTION

The principles and procedures which concern contested creditor's bankruptcy petitions are contained in various judgments and fine textbooks on personal insolvency. However, there are no books (as far as the authors are aware) which in one place deal exclusively with the legal and practical aspects of a contested creditor's bankruptcy petition.

So, this book aims to fill that gap by outlining the principles and procedures of contested bankruptcy petitions. It also aims to provide practical guidance wheresoever appropriate to the lawyer who is tasked with dealing with such a matter.

For the sake of completeness, this book is concerned with individuals in respect of whom the courts in England and Wales have jurisdiction to make a bankruptcy order. This is dealt with in s.265 of the Insolvency Act 1986[1] which provides:

> "(1) A bankruptcy petition may be presented to the court under section 264(1)(a) only if—
>
> (a) the centre of the debtor's main interests is in England and Wales, or
>
> (ab) the centre of the debtor's main interests is in a member State (other than Denmark) and the debtor has an establishment in England and Wales, or

[1] Hereafter, unless otherwise stated, references in this book to sections shall be references to the sections in the Insolvency Act 1986.

(b).. the test in subsection (2) is met.

(2) The test is that—

(a) the debtor is domiciled in England and Wales, or

(b) at any time in the period of three years ending with the day on which the petition is presented, the debtor—

(i) has been ordinarily resident, or has had a place of residence, in England and Wales, or

(ii) has carried on business in England and Wales."

Readers are accordingly advised to consult specialist works for individuals who fall outside the scope of the above provision.

CHAPTER TWO

WHY PRESENT A BANKRUPTCY PETITION?

There are many options available to the unpaid creditor besides seeking to make an individual bankrupt. Nonetheless, bankruptcy is an option which is still regularly chosen. This chapter seeks to explore why that may be; the point of this discussion is to enable lawyers to consider at an early stage whether they wish to advise their client(s) of proceeding with the presentation of a bankruptcy petition. This chapter assumes that the debt which is intended to form the basis of the petition is liquidated[2] (though that is no less a material consideration and the reader is advised to consider the discussion in Chapter 4).

(a) No / Insufficient Assets

The most obvious example is where a debtor is both cash and asset poor. A petition represents the only real way an unpaid creditor can hope to achieve *something* (often pence in the pound) rather than nothing.

We say *something* because an unpaid creditor must share rateably in an individuals' insolvent estate with other creditors. At its crudest – making an individual bankrupt is most unlikely to mean that you will be paid the full amount owed.

Typically, the most valuable asset an individual will own will be their family home; but obtaining a charge over the family home will be unattractive if there isn't sufficient equity in the property or if there are a

---

2 See s.267(2)(b) IA.

number of pre-existing charges which make the prospect of a return unlikely.

An income payments order may also be unattractive if the relevant individual's earning capacity is so low that repayment of the debt will take far too long.

(b) Pressure / Time & Cost Savings

It is true that, historically, courts have taken a very dim view of resorting to insolvency processes as a method of debt collection. However, it has been said (albeit in the context of corporate insolvency but no less applicable to personal insolvency) that it is not improper for a creditor with an undisputed debt to present a winding up petition in the hopes of inducing the creditor to pay.[3] There is no reason why that logic should not apply in cases of personal insolvency. So, when a party is owed an undisputed debt, the presentation of a bankruptcy petition may simply be the quickest and cheapest way of ensuring the creditor is 'taken seriously' and is paid what is due to them. In this way, contrary to what is said above, a party who is cash and asset rich may prove to be an attractive target for a bankruptcy petition because it may lead to swift payment by the debtor in the hope of avoiding a bankruptcy order.

However, a word of caution is necessary here. As will be explained in subsequent chapters, that logic does not apply in cases where a debt is genuinely disputed. In such circumstances, a petitioning creditor is vulnerable to indemnity costs being awarded against them when they present a petition based on a disputed debt. That is because it is an abuse of process to present a petition where the debt therein is genuinely

---

3 Sell Your Car With Us Ltd v Sareen [2019] EWHC 2332 (Ch); [2019] B.C.C. 1211 [53].

disputed.[4] Hence, a sensible practical step to take is to consider whether the debt claimed is capable of genuine dispute – in essence, an assessment of the merits is required (in the light, in particular, of any correspondence that has already been exchanged between creditor and debtor, or the parties' respective lawyers). Of course, the position may not be clear cut and in such circumstances the decision whether to proceed becomes a matter of overall likelihood of success and risk appetite.

The advantage of seeking a bankruptcy order in the case of an undisputed debt (or a debt which is not considered to be genuinely disputed) is that it saves much time and cost compared to commencing Part 7 litigation under the Civil Procedure Rules. To an aggrieved creditor (whose return will already be steadily decreasing on account of paying legal fees) that will likely be an attractive option.

---

4 Re Kirkman-Moeller [2005] BPIR 1136; [2005] EWHC 381 [8–11]; (Ch); Re a Company (No 0012209 of 1991) [1992] 1 WLR 351; [1992] 2 All E.R. 797 at 354

CHAPTER THREE

JURISDICTION

Introduction

This chapter is concerned with the territorial jurisdiction of the courts of England and Wales to hear a bankruptcy petition against a debtor. Jurisdiction is an issue that can be relevant both in relation to a debtor's own bankruptcy application, and also a creditor's bankruptcy petition. The law is stated in s. 236I (debtor's own application) and s. 265 (creditor's petition). The two sections are virtually identical. For convenience, this chapter refers to s. 265 in preference to s. 263I since s. 265 is encountered far more frequently in practice.

Overview

In order to establish that the courts of England and Wales have jurisdiction, it is necessary for the applicant or petitioner to demonstrate that one of the several jurisdictional "anchors" is made out. The "anchors" are alternative to each other. Strictly speaking, it is only necessary to demonstrate that one is made out, although strategically, a petitioner may wish to contend that more than one is made out. It is the applicant or petitioner that bears the burden of proof, as appropriate.

Where the issue of jurisdiction arises for example on an application to serve a bankruptcy petition out of the jurisdiction, the standard of proof that the petitioner must meet is that of a good arguable case.[5] A good

5 See the judgment of Deputy ICC Judge Kurl KC in Mobile Telecommunications Co KSCP v Al Saud [2023] EWHC 312 (Ch), [2023] BPIR 1179 at [22]–[34].

arguable case means that one side has a better argument than the other on the material available.[6]

Each of the "anchors" is addressed in turn below. Two of them (a debtor's centre of main interests or a debtor's establishment) are hang overs from the European regime for insolvency of which the United Kingdom was part until Brexit.

The sections are organised so that if a debtor's centre of main interest is either in England and Wales or in another member state of the European Union (other than Denmark) (and, in the case of the latter, the debtor also has an establishment in England Wales) then the courts of England and Wales have jurisdiction and it is not necessary to go any further. If, by contrast, the debtor has neither his centre of main interests, nor an establishment in England and Wales, then the other jurisdictional anchors come into play.

From a practical point of view, this means that a creditor is well advised to consider, first, whether it can be demonstrated that a debtor's centre of main interest is in England and Wales or in a European Union member state (other than Denmark).

Centre of Main Interests & Establishment

The concepts of centre of main interests (often referred to as COMI) and establishment are derived from EU law, first the Insolvency Regulation 2000 (EC) 1346/2000, and then the Recast Insolvency Regulation (EU) 2015/848.

The United Kingdom left the EU on 'exit day': 31 January 2020 at 11.00pm.[7] This was followed by a transition period that lasted until 31

---

6 Canada Trust Co v Stolzenberg (No 2) [1998] 1 W.L.R. 547.

7 s. 20(1) of the European Union (Withdrawal) Act 2018.

December 2020.[8] The law set out in this Chapter is the law as it applies following the end of the transition period. Moreover, the law set out in this Chapter is the law that will apply to petitions or applications presented after 31 December 2020, and where there are no insolvency proceedings against the debtor at that time in an EU member state.[9]

Both the original and the recast EU insolvency regulations were transplanted into the law of England and Wales at the end of the transition period. The Insolvency (Amendment) (EU Exit) Regulations 2019 / 146 made significant amendments to the Recast Insolvency Regulation (EU) 2015/848 as retained in the law of England and Wales. The regulation, as so amended, is referred to as the "Retained Insolvency Regulation".

A debtor's COMI is defined by the Retained Insolvency Regulation as *"… the place where the debtor conducts the administration of its interest on a regular basis and which is ascertainable by third parties"*.[10] There are some presumptions which can be applied to assist in determining the COMI. Relevantly to bankruptcy, if the debtor is an individual that exercised an independent business or professional activity, their COMI is presumed to be the debtor's principal place of business in the absence of proof to the contrary (provided that the debtor's principal place of business has not moved in the three month period prior to the presentation of the application or petition). If the debtor is not such an individual, then the presumption is that a debtor's COMI is their habitual residence

---

8 s. 39 of the European Union (Withdrawal Agreement) Act 2020.

9 If there were such proceedings (and provided that they are 'main proceedings'), then the effect of Article 67(3) of the Agreement on the withdrawal of the United Kingdom of Great Britain and Northern Ireland from the European Union and the European Atomic Energy Community is that the Recast Insolvency Regulation will apply to those proceedings.

10 Article 3 of the Retained Insolvency Regulation.

(provided that there has been on move of the habitual residence in the six-month period prior to the presentation of the application or petition).

According to the Retained Insolvency Regulation, a debtor has an establishment if they have "*any place of operations where a debtor carries out or has carried out in the 3-month period prior to the request to open insolvency proceedings a non-transitory economic activity with human means and assets.*"[11]

In order for the court to have jurisdiction on the basis of a debtor's COMI, it is necessary to demonstrate that the COMI was in England and Wales at the date of the presentation of the petition or application, rather than the date of the hearing.[12]

The court will consider a variety of factors when deciding whether a debtor's COMI is in England and Wales (or, for that matter, in another EU member state other than Denmark). It is perfectly permissible for a debtor to move their COMI, but their COMI must be ascertainable by third parties – in that sense, the search is for objective factors: for example, where is the place that a debtor can be contacted. A debtor's 'habitual residence' for these purposes is equated with their settled permanent home, the place where a debtor lives with family and return to from business trips. The word 'interests' as used in the definition is apt to encapsulate of course economic interests (commercial, financial and professional, but also consumer activity). Conducting the administration of one affairs normally connotes management and control of a debtor's affairs. The reference in the definition to a 'regular basis' imports some continuity or normality. A court can look at what the debtor did before

11 Article 2(10) of the Retained Insolvency Regulation.

12 See [42]-[43] of the decision of ICC Judge Greenwood in Portrait & Burns v Minai [2023] EWHC 1605 (Ch) [2023] B.P.I.R. 1205.

and after the presentation of the petition or application.[13] A debtor can only ever have one COMI.

In the authors' experience, the sort of evidence that is normally assembled and presented to the court includes evidence obtained from a debtor's social media accounts (for example showing where the debtor lives or is professionally based), documents tending to show a debtor's immigration status or residency rights (for example council tax bills or voter registrations or property ownership or tenancy documents). It is also common for a debtor to have to disclose their bank account statements, since this will show, in the case of habitual residence, where a debtor undertakes normal day-to-day spending.

If a debtor's COMI is an EU Member State (other than Denmark), then the courts of England and Wales will have jurisdiction if the debtor has an establishment in England and Wales. As with proving a debtor's COMI, proving that a debtor has an establishment is also a matter to be proved on the basis of objective factors that are ascertainable by third parties. According to the Supreme Court the search is for a fixed place of business, from which business activities which consist in dealings with third parties (rather than internal administration) take place. A brass name on a door is not likely to be sufficient.[14]

---

13 See [44] of Minai, and also Shierson v Vlieland-Boddy [2005] EWCA Civ 974, [2005] 1 WLR 3966.

14 The Trustees of the Olympic Airlines SA Pension and Life Assurance Scheme v Olympic Airlines SA [2015] UKSC 27 [2015] 1 W.L.R. 2399 at [13] as applied in Chen Yung Ngai Kenneth v Li Shu Chung [2021] EWHC 3346 (Ch) [2022] B.P.I.R 507. See also Trillium (Nelson) Properties Ltd v Office Metro Ltd [2012] EWHC 1191 (Ch) [2012] B.P.I.R. 1049 at [35]-[36].

Domicile

A debtor's domicile is a matter that must be proved to the ordinary civil balance of probabilities standard. In *Henwood v Barlow Clowes International Ltd (In Liquidation)*[15] the Court of Appeal summarised the relevant legal principles in relation to a person's domicile (at [8]). They include that a person can only ever have one domicile (and that each person has a domicile): this is either a domicile of origin or a domicile of choice. A person's domicile is in the country where they have their permanent home, or, as it has been put, the place where the person would want to spend their last days. In order to acquire a domicile of choice, a debtor would need to demonstrate a combination of residence along with proving that their intentions were to have a domicile in another country.

In order to determine a person's domicile, a court can have regard to any circumstance that is evidence of a person' residence or their intention to reside permanently or indefinitely in a particular country. This will include questions of motive, whether residence was freely chosen, and also whether a person's residence is precarious. In practice, a court will be wary of accepting self-serving statements by a debtor, particularly where they are contradicted by other evidence or not corroborated by the debtor's own actions. It is not necessary to prove that a person is a citizen of the country in which they claim to be domiciled.

Ordinarily resident or place of residence

A person's 'ordinary residence' is a question of fact and degree, it is not a legal term of art. A person can have more than one ordinary residence. The residence at the relevant place must have some degree of permanence. It is not sufficient to make occasional or casual visits. It must be occupied as a residence (not for a business). For a place to be an ordinary residence, the debtor must reside there for a substantial period

[15] [2008] EWCA Civ 577; [2008] B.P.I.R. 778

of time. For example, staying in a hotel room is unlikely to qualify as a person's ordinary residence, by contrast, where a person pays for exclusive use and does reside in a place, that may count as that person's ordinary residence. It is not a pre-condition that the person should be the landlord or tenant of the relevant space, nor that it is place in which a person lives with their family. On the other hand, the fact that a person possesses keys to a specific residence may be indicative that it is an ordinary residence.[16]

In deciding whether a person has a 'place of residence', the court is looking at a 'de facto' situation.[17] Some cases in the insolvency context borrow from tax law on the concept of a place of residence; in particular, by reference to the definition of 'reside', which includes to live in or at a particular place, and the need for the residence to have a degree of permanence and continuity.[18] Conversely, it is not necessary to establish that the debtor had a legal right to occupy the particular place of residence (it is thus not necessary to show that a debtor was a tenant or a licensee – a moral claim is sufficient). Indeed, having a legal right to occupy a particular place (but then not occupying it) is unlikely to qualify as a place of residence.[19]

Lastly, it is important to emphasise that the concepts of 'ordinarily resident' and 'place of residence' are different. Although as case law makes clear, that is not to say that factors which are relevant to one, might not

---

16 Reynolds Porter Chamberlain LLP v Khan [2016] B.P.I.R. 722, in particular at [25].

17 [2016] B.P.I.R 722 at [26], and Lakatamia Shipping Company Ltd v Su [2021] EWHC 1866 (Ch) [2021] Bus L.R. 1285.

18 [2021] EWHC 1866 (Ch) [34].

19 Mobile Telecommunications Company KSCP v Hrh Prince Hussam Bin Saud Bin Abdulaziz Al Saud [2025] EWHC 85 (Ch) [2025] B.P.I.R. 518 at [148].

also be relevant to the other, although it should not be assumed that all factors relevant to one are relevant to the other.[20]

Carried on business

The first point to make in relation to this head of jurisdiction is that it is necessary to prove that it was the debtor that was carrying on the business, not a company or LLP of which the debtor is a shareholder, director, or member[21] (for example, a debtor that is running his company's business is not running his own business, but rather they are running the company's business). That is not to say, however, that an individual that is involved in a number of companies may be treated by the court as themselves carrying on business as a promoter of companies.[22] The distinction is not an easy one to draw: for example, in Anglo Irish Bank Corporation Ltd v Flannery,[23] the court concluded that the debtor in that case was not carrying on business in England and Wales. He was a property developer, albeit living in Andorra, with international business interests, including some in England and Wales. Although he was a shareholder in various companies, he was not running them, and there was no evidence that he had promoted companies.

In *Darren Neil Masters v Barclays Bank Plc*[24] Norris J explained that whether a debtor is carrying on a business is a mixed question of fact and law[25]. A judge will first need to decide – as a matter of fact (and

[20] [2016] B.P.I.R 722 [27].

[21] Re Brauch (A debtor) [1978) Ch. 316. In this case, the debtor was involved in some 90 companies, and the court found that he was carrying on personally the business of promoting companies.

[22] Re Clark [1914] 3 K.B. 1095.

[23] [2013] B.P.I.R. 1

[24] [2013] EWHC 2166 (Ch) [2013] BPIR 1058,

[25] [2013] EWHC 2166 (Ch) [2013] BPIR 1058 [16]

considering the totality of the evidence) – what acts the debtor undertook. Then, second, the judge will need to decide whether those acts amount to carrying on a business.[26] The burden is on the person asserting that the debtor was carrying on a business; if it is a creditor's petition, then the burden is on the creditor[27]. A single transaction by an individual can constitute the carrying on of business[28], although it is necessary to consider carefully what activities the debtor has undertaken in the jurisdiction, and to contrast that with the activities undertaken outside the jurisdiction. In *Gate Gourmet Luxembourg IV Sarl v Morby,*[29] the court accepted that a transaction which amounted to selling shares in a group could amount to carrying on business.[30] Another way of looking at the matter may be to ask if the acts of the debtor do not amount to carrying on business, are they instead charitable work, or a pastime or hobby.

---

[26] See [43]-[44] of Jones v Aston Risk Management Ltd [2024] EWHC 2553 (Ch) [2025] B.P.I.R. 280 and Durkan v. Jones [2023] BPIR 1074.

[27] [2013] EWHC 2166 (Ch); [2013] BPIR 1058 [16(d)]

[28] [2013] EWHC 2166 (Ch) [2013] BPIR 1058 [20]

[29] [2015] EWHC 1203 (Ch); [2015] B.P.I.R. 787.

[30] An incomplete transaction would not, however, amount to carrying on business: Charlton v Funding Circle Trustee Limited [2019] EWHC 2701 (Ch); [2019] EWHC 2701 (Ch) [22]. In Charlton, the transaction was a potential share sale which did not complete.

CHAPTER FOUR

DISPUTING A BANKRUPTCY PETITION

This chapter will outline different ways a party may contest the making of a bankruptcy order by reference to both legislation and case law. It will, where appropriate, be interspersed with practical guidance.

Preliminary Considerations

As the court neatly summarised in *Revenue and Customs Commissioners v Potter*[31]

> *"Section 267(2) "provides conditions for the presentation of a petition, and materially that the debt is one 'which the debtor appears either to be unable to pay or to have no reasonable prospect of being able to pay'." Section 268 of the Act provides that condition (c) is only satisfied:*
>
> *'if, the debt is payable immediately and [relevant to this matter]—*
>
> *(a) the petitioning creditor to whom the debt is owed has served on the debtor a demand (known as "the statutory demand") in the prescribed form requiring him to pay the debt or to secure or compound for it to the satisfaction of the creditor, at least 3 weeks have elapsed since the demand was served and the demand*

[31] [2008] B.P.I.R. 1033 [25]

> *has been neither complied with nor set aside in accordance with the rules"*

The debt itself must be liquidated, owed to the petitioning creditor and equal to or in excess of the bankruptcy level, which is £5,000.[32]

The court has a discretion over whether to make a bankruptcy order, see r.10.24 of the Insolvency (England and Wales) Rules 2016.[33]

(a) Standing

It is logical to consider the question of standing first. If the petitioner does not have standing to present the petition, then the petition can proceed no further.

A creditor who is owed a debt capable of founding a petition will of course have standing.

However, that gives rise to questions of whether an individual is in fact a creditor at all; whilst that might appear to be a straightforward question there are nuances that fall to be considered.

Assignees

A debt which has been assigned in accordance with s.136 of the Law of Property Act 1925 entitles the assignee to present a petition without joining the assignor. The same appears to be true of an equitable assignee.[34]

---

32 If the petition is presented by more than one creditor, then the combined total of the debts owed must equal or exceed £5,000, see s.267(4) IA.

33 Hereafter referred to as IR.

34 Re Steel Wing Co Ltd [1921] 1 Ch 349 at 357.

Companies

A petition can be presented by a company in its own name. Where the company is in liquidation, the petition must be in the name of the Company[35] and should be followed by the words acting by its liquidator, [X].

Trustees in Bankruptcy

A trustee in bankruptcy may present a petition. Unlike corporate insolvency, the cause of action will vest in the trustee such that they are entitled to sue in their own name(s).

Partnerships

Partners suing in the partnership's name have the ability to present a petition.[36]

Receivers

Receivers are not entitled to present a petition in their own names for debts owed to the company over which they are appointed.[37] In such circumstances the chargor company is the creditor who must petition and in practice the styling is similar to companies in liquidation, see above. It is of course possible that the individual is owed a debt other than in their capacity as receiver, for instance if he is the assignee of a debt or holds a bill of exchange.[38]

---

35 Re Debtor (No.41 of 1951) [1952] Ch 192 ; [1952] 1 All E.R.107 at 195

36 *Schaw, Miller & Bailey: Personal Insolvency Law & Practice, 5th Ed* at [8.68]

37 Ex p. Sacker (1888) 22 Q.B.D. 179 at 856.

38 (1888) 22 Q.B.D. 179 at 856.

Creditor with Foreign Judgment Debt

A creditor with a foreign judgment which has not been the subject of separate recognition proceedings in England does not have standing to present a bankruptcy petition.[39]

(b) Disputed Debt

The most common basis for opposing a bankruptcy petition is that the debt is disputed. This relates to standing because the debtor in such cases is saying that the petitioner is not his creditor.

The test is whether the debt is genuinely disputed.[40]

The nature or the standard of the test is essentially the same which applies on an application for summary judgment under CPR Part 24. In short, the dispute raised must have a real prospect of success[41].

It is the same test which applies on an application to set aside a statutory demand under r.10.5(5)(b) IR. In the context of such an application, a party is able to demonstrate that a debt is disputed on substantial grounds by demonstrating that there is a genuine triable issue[42]. In this way,

39 Servis-Terminal LLC v Drelle [2025] EWCA Civ 62 ; [2025] B.P.I.R. 564 [55-56].

40 Go Capital Limited v Jagdeep Singh Phull [2020] EWHC 1235 ; [2020] B.P.I.R 819 [25]

41 Alexander-Thedotou v Michael Kyprianou and Co LLC [2016] EWHC 1493 (Ch) ; [2016] BPIR 1114 [11-12]

42 Mittal v RP Capital Explorer Master Fund [2014] BPIR 1537 [14]

judicial observations concerning a 'genuine triable issue' in the statutory demand context will also be applicable in the petition context.[43]

Mini-Trials & Disputed Facts

Because the test can be likened to the summary judgment test, the classic exposition of the principles in *Easyair Limited v Opal Telecom Limited*[44] and indeed other cases concerning summary judgment will apply.

One of those principles concerns disputed facts; there will often be factual disputes between the parties which in turn speak to whether the debt is disputed. As is the case with summary judgment, the court is not permitted to carry out a mini trial.

However, the court is permitted to analyse the evidence as a whole to assess the sustainability of the assertions made. As the court put it in *Chopra v Katrin Properties Ltd*[45]

> *"In determining whether the dispute is substantial, the court should not conduct a mini-trial but it is permissible to scrutinise the evidence presented to establish if it is sustainable. Following a submission that the court should be cautious as it is only too easy for a debtor to raise many objections and claim that the cannot be resolved without cross-examination, Patten J (as he then was) explained in Portsmouth v Alldays Franchising Ltd [2005] BPIR 1394 (Ch) at para12:*
>
> *"[t]he mere fact that a party in proceedings not involving oral evidence or cross examination asserts that certain things did or did not occur, is not sufficient in itself to raise a triable issue*

[43] [2020] EWHC 1235; [2020] B.P.I.R 819 [25]

[44] [2009] EWHC 339 (Ch)

[45] [2022] EWHC 2728 (Ch) ; [2023] B.P.I.R 626 [87]

> *That evidence inevitably has to be considered against the background of all the other admissible evidence and material in order to judge whether it is an allegation of any substance. Once the court considers that the evidence is reliable in that sense, and not some attempt to obfuscate the real issues by raising a series of hopeless allegations then it does, of course, become necessary to consider what the legal consequences of it are."*

Accordingly:

- where there are genuinely disputed facts of relevance which are sustainable on a review of the evidence as a whole, the court will ordinarily dismiss the petition because the place for those matters to be determined is at a trial rather than on a summary basis at a petition hearing.

- Equally, just because there are factual disputes does not automatically spell the end of a petition if the allegation lacks substance following a review of all the evidence before the court. As the court explained above, merely making an assertion that certain things did or did not occur will not by itself be sufficient to raise a triable issue. Equally, as is the case with summary judgment, it is open to a court to reject evidence if it is inherently implausible.[46]

In *Collier v. P & M.J. Wright Holdings*[47] Arden LJ (as she then was) discussed evidential considerations:

> "*In my judgment, the requirements of substantiality or (if different) genuineness would not be met simply by showing that the dispute is arguable. There has to be something to suggest that*

---

46 In Re Kerkar [2021] EWHC 3255; [2022] B.P.I.R 408. [34]

47 Collier v. P & M.J. Wright Holdings [2007] EWCA Civ 1329; [2007] B.P.I.R 1452 [21].

> *the assertion is sustainable. The best evidence would be incontrovertible evidence to support the applicant's case, but this is rarely available. It would in general be enough if there were some evidence to support the applicant's version of the facts, such as a witness statement or a document, although it would be open to the court to reject that evidence if it was inherently implausible or if it was contradicted, or was not supported, by contemporaneous documentation (see also per as Lawrence Collins LJ states in Ashworth at [34]). But a mere assertion by the applicant that something had been said or happened would not generally be enough if those words or events were in dispute and material to the issue between the parties."*

It is doubtful whether a mere witness statement would be sufficient – not if all it did was simply deny or assert that a given matter occurred as it would fall foul of the observations by Patten J in *Portsmouth* above.

The court is concerned with the credibility of the evidence as opposed to the amount of evidence produced[48]

> *"Nobody would say that the evidence in this case was jejune. It extends to nine thick volumes of affidavits and exhibits. But the credibility of evidence does not depend upon the number, of kilograms achieved on either side, and the two points which ultimately emerge are in fact quite short ones."*

The practical considerations are these:

- Parties should ensure that they produce as much documentary evidence (which is of substance) as possible to demonstrate whether there is substance to the factual dispute.

[48] Claybridge Shipping Company SA [1997] BCLC 572.

- The case should be reviewed in the round as to whether a party's given stance on a matter is logically consistent and, overall, is sustainable.

- Producing huge amounts of evidence will not assist if ultimately there is little to no substance in the underlying assertion.

(c) **Preliminary Assessment**

In Ciddy Limited v Anjana Natalia[49] ICC Judge Agnello KC (as she then was) dismissed a bankrupty petition based on a loan agreement on the basis that substantial grounds had been shown that the relationship was unfair pursuant to s.140A-C of the Consumer Credit Act 1974. It was argued by the petitioner that even if successful on an unfair relationship claim, there would in any event still be a sum due which would exceed the bankruptcy level. The judge declined to carry out a pre-assessment of what the County Court might order by way of relief pursuant to the provisions above:

> *"45. Before me, the Petitioner effectively invites me to determine that there must remain a liability under the terms of the loan agreement and that this can form the basis for the bankruptcy order. The sums said to be due and owing vary from being the standard interest, to the legal costs, to the receivership costs. The submission was also made that in any event there must be a sum due which exceeds the bankruptcy level of £5,000 and that is all the Petitioner needed to establish. In my judgment, this is the incorrect approach to this case. Having determined that the Debtor has established substantial grounds relating to her section 140A-C CCA 1974 claim, any sum which remains outstanding will be determined in those proceedings. It is not for me to predetermine exactly what sum would be due under those*

[49] [2025] EWHC 1616 (Ch)

proceedings. Unlike in Re Field there is no liquidated debt due because the actual sum of what, if anything, is due still needs to be determined by the County Court. What the Petitioner is effectively inviting me to do is to quantify what sum the County Court will determine is due. In my judgment, that type of assessment forms no part of the bankruptcy jurisdiction. As I have determined that the Debtor has a good arguable case in relation to both unfair relationship and also the unenforceability of the default interest provisions, then until those proceedings have been determined, the Petitioner is not entitled to seek from the bankruptcy court an assessment in the form of a preliminary summary assessment that under the loan agreement there must be at least a particular sum still due and owing. Such an approach is also unfair to the Debtor who may be able to pay whatever sum is determined due by the County Court but may face a higher sum under the current petition."[50]

It is important to be clear about precisely what this authority decides. It does not stand as authority for the proposition that if a petition debt is disputed on substantial grounds, then the court may not carry out an assessment of whether there would in any event be a sum due above the bankruptcy level. That is to put the matter too widely. The position is more nuanced than that. For instance, where a party raises a counterclaim, the court *is* required to carry out an assessment of whether the counterclaim exceeds or equals the petition debt (as is dealt with below).

Instead, *Ciddy* is applicable where the petition debt itself is disputed and not by the means of a counterclaim. In those circumstances, if satisfied that the debt is disputed on substantial grounds, then the bankruptcy courts will not carry out a preliminary assessment of whether there will still be a particular sum which is due and owing. In *Ciddy*, for instance,

[50] [2025] EWHC 1616 (Ch) [45]

the court declined to carry out the exercise which would be carried out by the county court under the Consumer Credit Act 1974.

That being said, in the authors experience, the court may still be more instinctively attracted toward an approach based on realism – particularly where, even on the best day in court, a debtor will be most unlikely to reduce the sums owing to below the bankruptcy level.

Liquidated Sum?

The petition must be founded upon a liquidated sum. Whilst this is a matter which should be kept distinct from whether the debt is disputed or not, if a sum is not liquidated, it cannot be the subject of a petition and the petition therefore falls to be dismissed.[51]

The court adopts a substance over form approach when determining whether a sum is liquidated or not.[52]

A liquidated sum is a sum that that is "*pre-ascertained" or "a specific amount which has been fully and finally ascertained", although that allows for calculation in accordance with a contractual formula or mere addition*"[53]. So, contractual machinery, which when operated will produce a figure gives rise to a liquidated sum.[54]

---

51 Dusoruth v Orca Finance [2022] EWHC 2346 (Ch); [2023] B.P.I.R. 68 [123].

52 *Watson & Baister: Bankruptcy: Law And Practice* [4.085]

53 [2022] EWHC 2346 (Ch); [2023] B.P.I.R 68 [123]

54 McGuinness v Norwich and Peterborough Building Society [2011] EWCA Civ 1286; [2012] B.P.I.R 145 [36]

Indeed, it has been held:[55]

> *107. No definition of "liquidated sum" is given in the statute but the concept has been considered both by the courts and in academic works. The Petitioner's case is straightforward. Mr Ashworth referred me to the concise summary of the principle given by Chief ICC Judge Briggs in Sandelson v Mulville [2019] EWHC 1620 (Ch) at paragraph 5:*
>
> *"To be liquidated the sum of money has to be 'a specific amount which has been fully and finally ascertained'. If a debt is subject to an account or a claim for damages it will not be liquidated: section 383 of the Act and see generally Personal Insolvency: Law and Practice fifth Edition at 8.35-8.39""*
>
> *To like effect is the statement in Law of Insolvency (5th Ed), at paragraph 6-047:*
>
> *"The decisive hallmark of a liquidated claim is that the process of quantification is already complete and there is an absence of any element of 'penalty' to be imposed over and above the actual loss sustained."*

A sum which requires a judicial process to determine its quantum (as is the case with damages) will not be a liquidated sum. Nor will there be a liquidated sum in the absence of a pre-ascertained liability under the contract or the existence of a contractual formula to produce a definite sum.

A liquidated sum can be said to exist where there is an admission, acknowledgment or agreement in respect of the quantification of a debt from which a debtor cannot resile:

[55] [2022] EWHC 2346 (Ch); [2023] B.P.I.R. 68. [107]

> *"...it does not matter whether the petitioner puts a figure on his claim, even if he can calculate it "down to the last penny". It must be liquidated either because the quantification of the debt is one from which the debtor is not permitted to resile as a matter of admission, acknowledgment or agreement, or because it has been determined as a matter of the court process."*[56]

A mere acknowledgment is insufficient to 'bind him to forego judicial assessment or determination' and instead 'an agreement for consideration or conduct giving rise to an estoppel according to established principles' is necessary.[57]

Examples of Liquidated Sums

By way of non-exhaustive example:

- Sums due under a loan agreement will give rise to a liquidated sum. That is because the quantification of the sums due will be pre-ascertained by the agreement itself.[58]

- Sums due under a guarantee which as a matter of construction give rise to a contingent payment obligation or concurrent liability with the debtor for what is due.[59] Guarantees are explored in a little further detail below.

- Judgment debts are of course liquidated sums as the figure has been fully and finally ascertained.

---

56 [2022] EWHC 2346 (Ch); [2023] B.P.I.R. 68. [123]

57 Truex v Toll [2009] EWHC 396 (Ch); [2009] B.P.I.R. 692 [36].

58 Khan v Singh-Sall & Anor [2023] EWCA Civ 1119; [2024] B.P.I.R 116 [25-29]

59 [2011] EWCA Civ 1286; [2012] B.P.I.R 145 [7-8]

- Monies due pursuant to an interim payments order by CPR r.25.6 amount to a liquidated sum[60]

- Sums due pursuant to an order for an interim payment on account of costs[61]

- Assessed costs bills[62]

- Unpaid council tax where there is a liability order[63]

- Unpaid council tax where there is no liability order[64]

- Unpaid rent[65]

- Sums due under a liquidated damages clause[66]

---

60 Maxwell v Bishopsgate Investment Management Ltd (In Liquidation) (No.2*)* [1993] T.L.R. 67

61 King v Bar Mutual Indemnity Fund [2023] EWHC 1408 (Ch); [2023] B.P.I.R 1386 (Ch) [64-67]

62 Klamer v Kyrkiakides and Braier (a firm) [2005] BPIR 1142 at 1147.

63 S.49 of the Council Tax (Administration and Enforcement) Regulations 1992 (SI 1992/613)

64 Bolsover DC v Ashfield Nominees Ltd [2010] EWCA Civ 1129; [2011] B.P.I.R. 7 [10]).

65 Hurley v Darjan Estate Co plc [2012] EWHC 189 (Ch); [2012] B.P.I.R. 1021 [6]

66 [2011] EWCA Civ 1286; [2012] B.P.I.R 145 [37]

- A solicitors unpaid intervention costs under the Solicitors Act 1974 Sch.1 para.13.[67]

Examples of Unliquidated Sums

- Claims for damages (or claims which on their true assessment produce only a remedy in damages).
- Claims under a guarantee which as a matter of construction give rise to an indemnity obligation or a 'see to it' obligation.[68]
- A restitutionary claim following unjust enrichment.[69]
- An unassessed solicitors' costs bill,[70] unless there has been an agreement to pay the sums claimed or the debtor is estopped from disputing the amounts sought (see above).[71]

Guarantees

Many petitions are brought against guarantors in respect of loan contracts between the principal debtor and the creditor.

In *McGuinness v Norwich and Peterborough Building Society*[72] it was held that a guarantee can impose upon a guarantor the following types of liability:

---

67 Law Society v Blavo [2018] EWCA Civ 2250; [2018] B.P.I.R. 1704

68 [2011] EWCA Civ 1286; [2012] B.P.I.R 145 [8]

69 [2022] EWHC 2346 (Ch); [2023] B.P.I.R. 68. [127]

70 [2005] B.P.I.R. 1142

71 Truex v Toll [2009] EWHC 396 (Ch) [36]

72 [2011] EWCA Civ 1286; [2012] B.P.I.R 145 [7]

(1) "a "see to it" obligation: i.e. an undertaking by the guarantor that the principal debtor will perform his own contract with the creditor;

(2) a conditional payment obligation: i.e. a promise by the guarantor to pay the instalments of principal and interest which fall due if the principal debtor fails to make those payments;

(3) an indemnity; and

(4) *a concurrent liability with the debtor for what is due under the contract of loan."*

The obligations in (2) and (4) create a liability in debt.[73]

Obligations in (3) give rise to a claim in damages.

A guarantee of the 'see to it' kind i.e. category (1) creates a liability in damages.[74]

Whilst a full assessment of the varied ways in which a guarantee can be disputed is outside the scope of this work, readers are advised to bear in mind the following:

- A guarantee is of course a contract, and so the usual defences to liability or means of asserting a contract is unenforceable will apply.

- Nowadays, it is the usual practice of lawyers to serve formal written demands on both the principal and the guarantor before serving a statutory demand/petition such that issues relating to

[73] [2011] EWCA Civ 1286; [2012] B.P.I.R 145 [8]

[74] [2011] EWCA Civ 1286; [2012] B.P.I.R 145 [8]

whether a demand needs to be served on such parties as a pre-requisite to enforcing guaranteed obligations seldom arise. As such, the issue is not explored in this book. Readers are advised to consult specialist texts on guarantees, and cases such as: *TS & S Global Ltd v Fithian-Franks*[75]); *MUR Joint Ventures BV & Compagnie Monesque De Banque*[76] *Martin* v *Mclaren Construction Ltd.*[77]

(d) Statute Barred Debts

No petition can be founded upon a debt which is statute barred. Close consideration will need to be given over whether the underlying claim is statute barred.[78]

(e) Judgment Debts / Tax Assessments / Council Tax

Judgment Debts

Judgment debts are generally irrefutable and amount to *prima facie* evidence that the debtor is indebted to the petitioning creditor.

There exists, however, an 'extraordinary'[79] jurisdiction of the bankruptcy court to go behind a judgment debt. It is important to bear in mind that

75 [2024] EWHC 1401 (Ch);

76 [2016] EWHC 3107 (Comm);

77 [2019] EWHC 2059 (Ch).

78 Mittal v RP Capital Explorer Master Fund [2014] B.P.I.R. 1537 [56-58]

79 Barclays Bank v Atay [2015] EWHC 3198 (Ch); [2016] B.P.I.R. 12 [12]

in doing so, the court is not setting aside the judgment, rather it 'goes round it'.[80]

To be clear, this jurisdiction is extraordinary – it is extremely rare for the court to be invited to exercise it, less still for the court to look behind a judgment.

In civil proceedings more generally, judgments may be set aside when obtained fraudulently,[81] or where there has been collusion.[82] Whilst a bankruptcy court will go behind a judgment in such circumstances[83] it's jurisdiction to do so extends beyond such circumstances. A bankruptcy court has jurisdiction to go behind a judgment when:

- *"satisfied that the judgment creditor manifestly had no claim against the judgment debtor on which the judgment could have been founded"*[84]

- When in relation to the judgment there is fraud, collusion or a miscarriage of justice. A miscarriage of justice was described as follows in *Dawodu v American Express Limited*[85]

> *"My only qualification to the summary by Warner J is that the cases establish that what is required before the court is prepared to investigate a judgment debt, in the*

---

[80] Re Fraser Ex parte Central Bank of London [1891-94] All ER Rep 939, at 941

[81] Royal Bank of Scotland plc v Highland Financial Partners LP [2013] EWCA Civ 328 [106]

[82] Bandon v Becher (1853) 3 Cl. & F. 479 at 510

[83] McCourt & Siequen v Baron [1997] BPIR 114, at 120

[84] [1997] BPIR 114 at 120

[85] [2001] BPIR 984 at 990

> *absence of an outstanding appeal or an application to set it aside, is some fraud, collusion, or miscarriage of justice. The latter phrase is of course capable of wide application according to the particular circumstances of the case. What in my judgment is required is that the court be shown something from which it can conclude that had there been a properly conducted judicial process it would have been found, or very likely would have been found, that nothing was in fact due to the claimant. It is clear that in those circumstances the court can inquire into the judgment and the judgment debt, even though the debtor himself has previously applied to have the judgment set aside, and even though that application has been refused and that refusal has been affirmed by the Court of Appeal – see In re Fraser; Ex parte Central Bank of London [1892] 2 QB 633"*

For an example of a case where the court refused to go behind a judgment debt, see *Barclays Bank v Atay.*[86]

Tax Assessments

A bankruptcy court does not have jurisdiction to review the manner in which an assessment was made or the merits thereto.[87] However, that should '*not to be taken to exclude the jurisdiction of the courts to decide a question of fact or law which is a basis for an income tax assessment where the taxpayer and the revenue so agree, provided the assessment to which the question relates has not become final and provided also the question, 'in form suitable for decision by the court', is not 'so close to the question of the assessment itself' that the court should decline to entertain it. But Lord*

86 [2015] EWHC 3198 (Ch); [2016] B.P.I.R 12.

87 Vieira v Revenue and Customs Commissioners [2017] EWHC 936 (Ch); [2017] B.P.I.R. 1062 [64]

Wilberforce was at pains to add that either the taxpayer or the revenue have the right to insist the statutory procedure should be followed'.[88]

Accordingly, the bankruptcy courts will not go behind a tax assessment the court will make a bankruptcy order "*unless, exceptionally, there is sufficient evidence that the assessment is fraudulent or collusive or that there has been some other glaring miscarriage of justice.*"[89]

Appeals?

If there is an extant appeal of the assessments before the tax courts, then the court has a discretion to adjourn (or dismiss the petition, though this seems extremely unlikely) if the appeal has a real prospect of success.[90]

At the petition stage, if a party is out of time for appealing then, the position is as stated above, i.e the court will make a bankruptcy order unless there is evidence of fraud, collusion or a miscarriage of justice.[91]

The position was neatly summarised in *Viera*[92]

> *"84. Turning to the Bankruptcy Court's discretion when considering a petition, I agree with counsel for HMRC that it is wider than when considering whether to set aside a statutory demand, but how wide it is depends on the taxpayer's position with regard to an appeal. If the taxpayer has exhausted his rights of appeal against the tax assessment or is out of time for*

88 Autologic Holdings Plc v Inland Revenue Commissioners [2005] UKHL 54; [2006] 1 A.C. 118 [14]

89 [2017] EWHC 936 (Ch); [2017] B.P.I.R. 1062 [84]

90 [2017] EWHC 936 (Ch); [2017] B.P.I.R. 1062 [84]

91 [2017] EWHC 936 (Ch); [2017] B.P.I.R. 1062 [84]

92 [2017] EWHC 936 (Ch); [2017] B.P.I.R. 1062 [84]

appealing, then the extent of the court's discretion is that stated in Lam and Chamberlin : the court will make a bankruptcy order unless, exceptionally, there is sufficient evidence that the assessment is fraudulent or collusive or that there has been some other glaring miscarriage of justice. If, on the other hand, the taxpayer has an extant appeal pending before the FTT, then D & D Marketing and Changtel show that the court's discretion is broader. In those circumstances, a key factor in the exercise of the court's discretion is whether the court considers that the appeal has a real prospect of success. If the court is satisfied that the appeal has no real prospect of success, then the court should make a bankruptcy order. Otherwise, the court may either adjourn the petition or dismiss it depending on the circumstances."

Council Tax

It has already been stated that sums due under a liability order amount to a debt for the purposes of s.267.

It can be the case that an individual initiates the appeal process or indeed makes an appeal to the Valuation Tribunal under s.16 of the Local Government Finance Act 1992. For the meaning of initiating the appeal process, see s.16(4)(7) which lays down various requirements that need to be satisfied before a party can appeal to the Valuation Tribunal.

At the hearing of a petition, there are conceivably five scenarios that can occur in relation to the underlying council tax liability:

(1) an appeal has been made to the Valuation Tribunal but has not yet been determined;

(2) no appeal has been made to the Valuation Tribunal;

(3) the appeal process has been initiated but the conditions necessary to proceed to appeal to the Valuation Tribunal have not yet been triggered;

(4) the appeal to the Valuation Tribunal was successful;

(5) the Appeal to the Valuation Tribunal was unsuccessful.

Category 1 – Appeal Not Yet Determined

The position is as stated in *Yang v Official Receiver:*[93]

> *"23. However, Lord Justice Hoffmann went on to say that if a debtor had a bona fide appeal, or an application to set aside the judgment, in existence at the time when the petition came on to be heard, it was the invariable practice to adjourn the hearing of the petition until that application or appeal had been decided. In my judgment, that is the appropriate way of dealing with a challenge to a liability order in respect of unpaid council tax on the hearing of the petition. If there is pending an appeal to the valuation tribunal, then the debtor can ask for the hearing of the petition to be adjourned pending the final determination of that appeal...."*

And *Okon v London Borough of Lewisham:*[94]

> *"22.I entirely agree with the above summary, and it is in my view entirely consistent with the subsequent Piggin case. In my judgment, the issue before the Judge at the hearing on 9 June 2015 was whether the Applicant's intended appeal to the valuation tribunal was bona fide and substantial and whether in the exercise of her discretion she ought to adjourn the*

93 [2013] EWHC 3577 (Ch); [2014] B.P.I.R 826 [23]

94 [2016] EWHC 864 (Ch); [2016] B.P.I.R 958 [22]

> *bankruptcy petition in order to await the outcome of that appeal."*

It is respectfully suggested that bona fide and substantial is the same standard as the test for disputing a bankruptcy petition, i.e the summary judgment standard.

Indeed, in *Re a Debtor (No.799 of 1994) ex parte Cobbs Property Services Ltd*[95] Harman J said:

> *'...the test advanced by Mr Patchett-Joyce which in my judgment is the correct way to look at the matter for the purpose of the registrar considering whether to exercise the power which he has to adjudicate upon the bankruptcy petition or whether to adjourn that petition pending an appeal, must turn upon the registrar's consideration as to whether the appeal was serious and whether the appeal was being taken seriously. Mr Patchett-Joyce's words are, in my opinion, entirely apt. Serious appeals are real appeals, to use Cotton LJ's phrase, and could be called bona fide appeals; that is, appeals properly worth considering and raising a point of law or other relevant appellate ground of substance.'*

In this regard it is also necessary to demonstrate that the appeal is being pursued seriously, as in *Cobbs*[96] it was said:

> *"The second half of Mr Patchett-Joyce's test, was the appeal being taken seriously?, is also appropriate...It is an appropriate test because, even if there be a point of substance on appeal, if the debtor seeking the adjournment of the bankruptcy hearing because of the appeal is not prosecuting his appeal with proper diligence, that is, taking it seriously, it can be said that he does*

95 [1995] 1 WLR 467 at 470

96 [1995] 1 WLR 467 at 470

> *not seem to think much of his appeal, and whatever the court may think of it, if the debtor is not prosecuting it seriously, the court should not allow the bankruptcy petition to be affected by it.'*

Accordingly:

- it is typically the case that the court will adjourn where there is an outstanding appeal which is bona fide and is being pursued seriously;
- lawyers acting for debtors should consider agreeing an adjournment with the petitioning creditor when there is an extant appeal outstanding.

Category 2 – No Appeal To The Valuation Tribunal

In *Choudhry v Luton*[97] a debtor had failed to do anything about liability orders and the High Court upheld a bankruptcy order made by the County Court:

> *"18. Going beyond that, it seems to me that the district judge could not anyway have concluded on the basis of the materials before him that there was a bona fide and substantial intended appeal to the valuation tribunal. Aside from the fact that Mr Choudhry did not raise the possibility in the hearing and had not previously taken any steps to challenge the liability orders, despite on any view having been aware of them for a matter of months, there simply was no evidence from which the district judge could conclude that a substantial challenge could be made. All that really bore on that was the first paragraph of the witness statement which took matters very little further."*

[97] [2017] EWHC 960 (Ch); [2017] B.P.I.R 1150 [18]

In short, where no steps whatsoever have been taken to challenge a liability order, then the petitioning creditor is in possession of an enforceable debt which can only be impeached if there is fraud or miscarriage of justice.[98]

Category 3 – Appeal Initiated But Not Yet Before Valuation Tribunal

The appeal process is set out in s.16 of the Local Government Finance Act 1992 and is (so far as relevant):

> "(1) A person may appeal to a valuation tribunal if he is aggrieved by—
>
> (a) any decision of a billing authority that a dwelling is a chargeable dwelling, or that he is liable to pay council tax in respect of such a dwelling; or
>
> (b) any calculation made by such an authority of an amount which he is liable to pay to the authority in respect of council tax.
>
> (2) In subsection (1) above the reference to any calculation of an amount includes a reference to any estimate of the amount.
>
> (3) Subsection (1) above shall not apply where the grounds on which the person concerned is aggrieved fall within such category or categories as may be prescribed.
>
> (4) No appeal may be made under subsection (1) above unless—

98 Yang v Official Receiver [2017] EWCA Civ 1465; [2018] B.P.I.R 255 [55]

> (a) the aggrieved person serves a written notice under this subsection; and
>
> (b) one of the conditions mentioned in subsection (7) below is fulfilled.
>
> (5) A notice under subsection (4) above must be served on the billing authority concerned.
>
> (6) A notice under subsection (4) above must state the matter by which and the grounds on which the person is aggrieved.
>
> (7) The conditions are that—
>
> (a) the aggrieved person is notified in writing, by the authority on which he served the notice, that the authority believes the grievance is not well founded, but the person is still aggrieved;
>
> (b) the aggrieved person is notified in writing, by the authority on which he served the notice, that steps have been taken to deal with the grievance, but the person is still aggrieved;
>
> (c) the period of two months, beginning with the date of service of the aggrieved person's notice, has ended without his being notified under paragraph (a) or (b) above.

If the relevant conditions in s.16(7) have not been triggered, for instance, if the individual hasn't yet been notified but two months have yet to expire, then in the author's view, whilst there would be no pending appeal, the court is more likely than not to adjourn the petition. Support for this line of thinking is taken from *Choudhury* above. It will be necessary to establish as above that the appeal is intended to be pursued and the same is substantial and bona fide.

Category 4 & 5– Successful Appeal / Unsuccessful Appeal

If the appeal is successful then the liability falls away and the petition falls to be dismissed.

If the appeal is unsuccessful, then unless fraud or a miscarriage of justice is shown the liability orders stand.

(f) Appeal Against Refusal to set aside statutory demand?

An outstanding appeal against the dismissal of an application to set aside a statutory demand does not prevent a party from presenting a bankruptcy petition and logically therefore cannot prevent the court from making a bankruptcy order.[99]

Although on the hearing of a petition the court will be unlikely to overlook the fact that there is an appeal pending. Although there is no authority on this point as far as the authors are aware, the court's approach is likely to be the same as above and below i.e, the court may adjourn if persuaded that the appeal has a real prospect of success and is being pursued seriously, that is with all due diligence.

(g) Counterclaim / Set-off/ Cross Demand

It is of course possible to dispute a bankruptcy petition on the basis that a debtor has a counterclaim/set-off/cross demand.[100]

---

99 Ahmad v Inland Revenue Commissioners [2004] EWHC 2292 (Ch); [2005] B.P.I.R. 541 [7]

100 Kaupthing Singer & Friedlander Ltd v Coomber [2011] EWHC 3589; [2012] B.P.I.R 774 (Ch)

The counterclaim etc must either extinguish the petition debt entirely or otherwise reduce it to below the £5,000 bankruptcy level and this is a matter which the court is required to consider.[101]

The counterclaim etc must have a real prospect of success.[102]

There must be mutuality, that is to say the legal character in which the debtor seeks to advance the counterclaim or cross-claim must be the same legal character that they are said to be liable to the petitioner. As the court helpfully explained in *Hurst v Bennet:*[103]

> *"11. In this context mutuality means that the legal character in which the creditor is or may be liable to the debtor by virtue of the counterclaim or cross-claim raised by the debtor is the same as the legal character in which the creditor is entitled to the debt the subject of the statutory demand. It does not mean that the claims have to arise out of the same contract or transaction. An example of a situation in which there is no mutuality is where a person brings a claim in his personal right and the defendant seeks to set off a claim against him in his capacity as a trustee for others. But the courts are prepared in certain situations to look at the reality of the situation, as Rimer J was prepared to do: see also for example Re Chapman ex parte Parker (1887) 4 Morr. 109 , where a defaulting trustee of a will was entitled to set off against a claim by the continuing trustees the amount to which he was entitled as a residuary legatee."*

101 Jeffrey Green Russell (A Firm) v Ruddock [2005] EWHC 3498 (Ch)

102 Ashworth v Newnote Limited [2007] EWCA Civ 793; [2007] B.P.I.R. 1012 [33]

103 [2001] EWCA Civ 182; [2001] B.P.I.R 287 [11]

Where the counterclaim etc is based on a clause within a contract, the clause in question must be capable of being enforced.[104]

A party cannot rely upon a claim against a third party as a basis for seeking the dismissal of a petition.[105]

(h) Pending Application For Permission to Appeal/ Pending Appeal Against a Judgment?

By r.10.24(2) IR:

> *"If the petition is brought in relation to a judgment debt, or a sum ordered by any court to be paid, the court may stay or dismiss the petition on the ground that an appeal is pending from the judgment or order, or that execution of the judgment has been stayed."*

Where there is a pending appeal against the judgment, the court should consider whether the appeal has a reasonable prospect of success.[106]

In *Re a Debtor (No.799 of 1994) ex parte Cobbs Property Services Ltd*[107] the court considered that it needed also to be shown that the appeal was bona fide and substantial and was being pursued seriously:

> *"That has been followed and applied in cases more recently, and the test advanced by Mr. Patchett-Joyce, which in my judgment is the correct way to look at the matter for the purpose of the registrar considering whether to exercise the power which he has*

---

104 Re A Debtor (No 35 of 2000) [2002] BPIR 75 at [7]

105 Inbakamar v United Trust Bank Ltd [2012] EWHC 845 (Ch); [2012] B.P.I.R 758 [37-39]

106 Westminster City Council v Parkin [2001] BPIR 1156, at 1158

107 [1995] 1 WLR 467 at 470

> *to adjudicate upon the bankruptcy petition or whether to adjourn that petition pending an appeal, must turn upon the registrar's consideration as to whether the appeal was serious and whether the appeal was being taken seriously. Mr. Patchett-Joyce's words are, in my opinion, entirely apt. Serious appeals are real appeals, to use Cotton L.J.'s phrase, and could be called bona fide appeals, that is, appeals properly worth considering and raising a point of law or other relevant appellate ground of substance.*
>
> *The second half of Mr. Patchett-Joyce's test, was the appeal being taken seriously?, is also appropriate, although not expressly or separately addressed in the earlier cases. It is an appropriate test because, even if there be a point of substance on appeal, if the debtor seeking the adjournment of the bankruptcy hearing because of the appeal is not prosecuting his appeal with proper diligence, that is, taking it seriously, it can be said that he does not seem to think much of his appeal, and whatever the court may think of it, if the debtor is not prosecuting it seriously, the court should not allow the bankruptcy petition to be affected by it."*

Parkin appears to suggest that the standard is slightly lower than on an application for summary judgment, given the reference to a 'reasonable prospect of success'. However, that was not the subject of argument and no party appeared for the other side so *Parkin* cannot be regarded, technically, as authority. It has, however, been given tentative endorsement in *Rehman v Boardman.*[108] It is respectfully suggested that rather than creating a sub-division of the appropriate standard to apply, the court was more likely thinking of the summary judgment test and given that that test is well known to courts, that is the test which the court will likely apply.

---

108 [2004] BPIR 820

Practical Considerations

- An assessment should be carried out of whether the pending appeal is bona fide and substantial.

- Evidence should also be directed to why the appeal is being pursued seriously, that is, with proper diligence, or not as the case may be.

Application For Permission To Appeal Pending

R.10.24(2) IR does not apply when an application for permission to appeal is pending. It is, however, a factor which the court can take into account as part of its discretion under r.10.24(1) IR.[109]

Permission And Appeal Application To Be Heard Together

When the application for permission to appeal and the appeal itself are intended to be heard together, in *Barker* the court construed *Rehman v Boardman*[110] to this effect:

> *[34] Mr Justice Lewison was taken to Parkin and noted that Arden J (who only had one party appearing before her) was concerned with an application for permission to appeal 'rather than a pending appeal'. Arden J had not been addressed on or taken to r 6.25(2) but Lewison J thought that her approach 'may well be appropriate' as the substantive appeal and permission application were to be heard together. The permission application and appeal effectively became one. In my view Lewison J retained the distinction between a pending appeal and an application for permission. The position was not too*

---

109 Barker v Baxendale-Walker [2018] EWHC 1681 (Ch); [2018] BPIR 1243 at [38-39]

110 [2018] EWHC 1681 (Ch); [2004] BPIR 820 [34]

> *dissimilar in Shotley Point Marina (1986) Ltd v Spalding [1997] 1 EGLR 233 where the Court of Appeal heard the combined application and made a decision on the merits of the appeal, taking into account any prejudice to the landlord. The approach taken by the Court of Appeal was efficient and practical. The case of Shotley Point Marina was referred to by Lewison J in Rehman.*

Accordingly, it has been suggested that the court will follow the approach of whether the appeal has a reasonable prospect of success.[111]

(i) Lack of utility?

Under s.266(3) the court has a discretion over whether to dismiss a petition.

That discretion can be exercised in cases where a bankruptcy order would serve no purpose because a debtor has no assets and no prospect of assets coming into existence.[112]

Mr Justice Snowden (as he then was) accepted the following propositions in *Maud:*[113]

> *"Secondly, the test is whether there is no possibility of any benefit to creditors. Thirdly, that the impossibility of benefit must be obvious at the petition hearing without any detailed*

[111] https://www.33bedfordrow.co.uk/print-insight?id=143:Article&printpage=true

[112] See Maud v Aabar Block S.a.r.L Edgeworth Capital (Luxembourg) S.a.r.L. [2016] EWHC 2175 (Ch) and Re Betts [1897] 1 Q.B; Shepherd v The Legal Services Commission [2003] BPIR 140; see also Re Thulin [1995] 1 WLR 165.

[113] Re Maud [2020] EWHC 974 (Ch) [114-117]

> *investigation. Fourthly, the concept of benefit includes a reasonable desire on the part of creditors that there should be an investigation by the trustee in bankruptcy."*

Even where it is established that a debtor neither has nor will have any assets, the court may well consider it appropriate to make a bankruptcy order so that the debtors affairs may be investigated.[114]

A debtor faces a heavy burden in showing that: they neither have nor will acquire any assets; and that *no useful investigation of the bankrupt's assets and affairs can be undertaken in the bankruptcy.*[115]

As regards the debtor's evidence in this respect, it is clear "*that the courts will not simply accept an uncorroborated statement by the debtor that he has no assets or that a bankruptcy order would serve no purpose.*"[116]

Hence, documentary evidence will be required, such as bank statements, documents demonstrating the ownership of property for instance.

One cannot say that there is no point in making a bankruptcy order because the fees and expenses of the bankruptcy will swallow any return to creditors.[117]

(j) Offer of Security / to Compound?

By s.271(3)

---

[114] Shepherd v The Legal Services Commission [2003] BPIR 140

[115] Harriet Lock v Aylesbury Vale District Council [2018] EWHC 2015 (Ch); [2018] B.P.I.R 1694 [35]

[116] Re Glenn Maud Edgeworth Capital (Luxembourg) SARL and another v Maud [2020] EWHC 974 (Ch); [2020] B.P.I.R 903 [117]

[117] In re Jubb Ex parte Burman and Greenwood. [1897] 1 Q.B. 641 at 643

> *"The court may dismiss the petition if it is satisfied that the debtor is able to pay all his debts or is satisfied–*
>
> *(a) that the debtor has made an offer to secure or compound for a debt in respect of which the petition is presented,*
>
> *(b) that the acceptance of that offer would have required the dismissal of the petition, and*
>
> *(c) that the offer has been unreasonably refused;*
>
> *and, in determining for the purposes of this subsection whether the debtor is able to pay all his debts, the court shall take into account his contingent and prospective liabilities."*

For the purposes of an offer to secure or compound, the test is whether no reasonable hypothetical creditor would have rejected the debtor's offer,[118] The relevant principles as regards s.271(3) were laid down in *Garwood*[119] and are these:

> *"1. The starting point is to ask whether a reasonable hypothetical creditor in the position of a petitioning creditor would accept or refuse the offer, bearing in mind, however, that there could be a range of reasonable positions that such a creditor could adopt.*
>
> *2. The test is objective.*
>
> *3. It is necessary to consider the extent to which the reasonable hypothetical creditor may be taken to have the characteristics of a petitioning creditor.*

[118] HMRC v Garwood [2012] BPIR 575

[119] [2012] BPIR 575

> *4. The court must look at the position at the date of the hearing.*
>
> *5. The court is not limited to considering the matters taken into account by the petitioning creditor when the offer of security was refused. It must look at all the relevant factors and their impact on the reasonable hypothetical creditor.*
>
> *6. That includes the history.*
>
> *7. The debtor must be full, frank and open in providing the necessary information to enable the creditor to make an informed decision.*
>
> *8. A rigid institutional policy of rejecting offers to secure could be a relevant consideration, since the reasonable hypothetical creditor was obliged to consider an offer on its merits. Coherent in-house policies, however, are not necessarily wrong.*
>
> *9. A creditor is entitled to have regard to his own interests and is not obliged to take a chance or to show patience or generosity.*
>
> *10. The costs and resources implications for the creditor are a highly material consideration.*"

For an offer to amount to an offer for the purposes of s.271 IA it must be a concrete offer capable of acceptance – a present offer, not the possibility of a future offer. Security is only of value if it enables a debt to be paid within a reasonable time.[120]

The same logic applies to offers to pay – such offers should enable a debt to be paid within a reasonable time.

---

[120] Hughes and another v Howell [2021] EWCA Civ 1431; [2022] B.P.I.R. 135 [25].

The term 'compound' indicates that the offer does not have to be one which involves payment of the petition debt in full. The court has further suggested that:

> *"I do not suggest that an offer must always fully satisfy the bankruptcy debt in order for the court to conclude that its rejection by a creditor is unreasonable, but this is not the case upon which to pronounce upon what level of shortfall might lead to such a conclusion; inevitably it will be a fact specific issue."*[121]

In practice, though, an offer to compound which engenders a significant shortfall is likely to lead to the conclusion that the rejection of an offer is not unreasonable. Of course, if the shortfall is very low then it may be thought that refusal of the offer is unreasonable since acceptance of the offer would (all things being equal) lead to a better return than if the debtor is adjudged bankrupt. Practically, such circumstances are unlikely to arise because if the shortfall is low, a debtor would usually be able to top up the same from other sources.

The following are examples of cases where the court has not found a creditor's refusal unreasonable:

- In *Barclays Bank Plc v Atay*[122] a debtor's offer to compound a debt by paying instalments over 15 years and where he had defaulted on similar agreements in the past;

- In *Cooke v Dunbar Assets Plc*[123] a debtor's offer of the half-share of equity in his matrimonial home, amounted to less than a

---

[121] Cooke v Dunbar Assets Plc [2016] EWHC 579 (Ch); [2016] B.P.I.R 576 [41]

[122] [2015] EWHC 3198 (Ch)

[123] [2016] EWHC 579 (Ch); [2016] B.P.I.R 576

quarter of his liability to the creditor and there would be real difficulties in realising the half-share;

- In *Sahota v Singh*[124] a creditor's refusal to take an assignment of a costs order against a party resident in India, in circumstances where the proposed assignor had not sought to enforce the debt in the six years since obtaining the costs order.

Offers of security should be sufficiently detailed to enable a petitioner to make an informed assessment of whether to accept the offer. The more information which is provided – the better.

Heidi Boulton v Queen Margaret's School York Limited[125] is a rare example of a case where the court found a creditor's rejection of an offer unreasonable. The debtor offered to repay the full amount of the undisputed element of the debt plus 3% interest above base rate in four months. The debtor further offered a charge over a property with ample equity. The court accepted the following reasons given on why the creditor's rejection was unreasonable:

> "*(1) The instalment payments by Mr Stalker were only scheduled to last a few months before the petitioner would be paid in full.*
>
> *(2) A large part of the debt had already been paid in January/February 2018, that is to say, the first instalment of £10,000 by Mr Stalker.*
>
> *(3) There was evidence adduced in support of the third party's ability to make payments by instalment, that is to say, the letter from Suffolk Petroleum Services Ltd.*

---

124 [2018] EWHC 2646 (Ch)

125 [2018] EWHC 3729 (Ch) [33]

(4) There would be no obligation on Mr Stalker to make payments to discharge the debt owed to the petitioner in the course of a bankruptcy.

(5) All documentation relating to the consents needed from the chargee and the appellant's mother had been provided by 7 March 2018.

(6) The evidence before the court was that there was significant equity in the property of around £200,000 and, accordingly, ample security for the petitioner.

(7) There was an obvious advantage to the petitioner being a secured as opposed to an unsecured creditor.

(8) The appellant had offered to pay interest on the undisputed element of the petition debt at the rate of 3 percent above base.

(9) The petitioner's stance of demanding payment of the disputed part of the petition debt and its costs on the indemnity basis was unreasonable."

Practical Guidance

- Offers of security should be sufficiently detailed to enable a petitioner to make an informed assessment of whether to accept the offer. The more information which is provided – the better.

- Offers to compound should provide for the debt to paid within as short a time as possible.

(k) Assertion of solvency?

A debtor cannot avoid a bankruptcy order being made by demonstrating that he or she is solvent.[126]

(l) Payment in full

It has been suggested that the opening words of s.271(3) are now of little utility and that a debtor need simply pay a petitioning creditors debt, unless a change of carriage order is made.[127]

(m) Adjournment – Time To Pay

The court has the power to adjourn a bankruptcy petition. That power will be exercised when there is credible evidence that there is a reasonable prospect that the petition debt will be paid within a reasonable time.[128]

Broadly speaking the court is not typically inclined towards granting long or repeated adjournments.[129]

The court's approach towards such an application is best encapsulated as follows: "*in order to secure such an adjournment a debtor must be ready to provide convincing evidence that the debt will be paid within a reasonable period*".

---

[126] [2007] EWHC 3325 (Ch)

[127] *Muir Hunter on Personal Insolvency,* Volume 1 [3-419].

[128] Edginton v Sekhon [2015] EWCA Civ 816; [2015] B.P.I.R 1397 [19]

[129] Garrow v Society of Lloyds [2000] 1 BCLC 10

In addition to the credibility of the evidence which will be the key consideration, other factors (on a non-exhaustive basis and depending on the facts) which the court can take into account are these:

(1) The timing of the application – in *Edginton* the court said:

> *"22. Delay is inimical to all forms of litigation and especially so in a collective enforcement process such as insolvency. In my judgment, the judge was entitled to take into account the very late stage which the application was made. Even in ordinary civil litigation, late applications are frowned upon, as are applications for adjournments which delay the final resolution of the case."*[130]

(2) the history of the matter/petition and of any broken promises[131] / opportunities afforded by successive adjournments;[132]

(3) the prima facie right of a petitioning creditor to obtain a bankruptcy order on a properly presented petition;

(4) delay more generally –

> *"Third, there is no indication that the registrar attached any or sufficient weight to the importance in bankruptcy proceedings of the court ensuring that delays are avoided or minimised once bankruptcy proceedings have been instituted. A primary purpose of such proceedings is to enable an independent person (the official receiver and subsequently the trustee) to ascertain and preserve all the assets of the debtor and to ascertain who are the creditors*

---

[130] [2015] EWCA Civ 816; [2015] B.P.I.R 1397 [22]

[131] Ross v Revenue and Customs Commissioners [2010] EWHC 13 (Ch); [2010] 2 All E.R. 126 [38]

[132] [1984] 1 WLR 1143 at 1149.

> *and in what amounts, with a view to the fair distribution of the assets to the creditors and the payment, so far as possible, of the sums owing to them, pari passu. The longer the delay through adjournments the greater the difficulties and anomalies."*[133]

It should also be noted that where there are supporting creditors, a debtor '*would need to provide credible evidence of his ability to pay within a reasonable time both the petition debt and the debt due to the supporting creditors*'.[134] Presumably that would not apply where the supporting creditor's debt is *bona fide* disputed, albeit in practice, there is unlikely to be any evidence before the court which enables that determination to be made.

Practical Guidance

- In practice, such applications are not made by way of formal application notice; rather a debtor will simply produce a witness statement and supporting exhibit. The application will then effectively be made orally. That is no incitement to laxity – strictly speaking, a formal insolvency act application should be made.

- In practice, the evidence submitted in support of being able to pay the petition debt within a reasonable time should be clear, detailed and cogent. Documentary evidence should almost always be provided lest the petitioner and indeed the court approach the matter with scepticism. The bankruptcy courts are no stranger to hearing repeated promises that a given transaction is very shortly due to complete which will enable the release of funds to pay the

---

133 [1984] 1 WLR 1143 at 150.

134 Robertson v Wojakovski [2020] EWHC 2737 (Ch); [2021] B.P.I.R 178 [15]

petition debt, for example. Generally, the court's patience is limited and in practice will eventually give way to scepticism.

- Vague evidence presents real problems; the court is unable to properly consider whether there is a reasonable prospect that the petition debt will be paid in a reasonable time such that the test will not be satisfied.

- It has been impliedly suggested that it is theoretically possible for a debtor to obtain an adjournment without producing any evidence:

  > "If the debtor does not produce any evidence of his ability to pay, he takes the risk that the court will not accept his bare assertion as to his means and ability to pay."[135]

  However, that cuts against the notion of there being credible evidence and, in any event, as a matter of practice is almost certainly likely to be dismissed by the court.

- In terms of what amounts to a reasonable time, that will be fact specific where the size of the debt will of course be material. Generally, a proposal which envisions the payment of only a modest sum in a very long time will be unreasonable.[136]

- In practice, what tends to occur is that at the first hearing (which often only has a very short time estimate in any event), the court will usually (unless it is plain that the test will not be satisfied) grant an adjournment. That will boil down to the court simply

---

[135] [2015] EWCA Civ 816; [2015] B.P.I.R 1397 [19]

[136] Gravesham Borough Council v Miss Titilayo Orebanwo [2020] EWHC 107 (Ch).

wishing to give the debtor at least one chance of avoiding the very severe and undesirable consequences of bankruptcy. This is by no means an immutable rule of practice and approaches will vary – it is however a useful rule of thumb.

(n) Interim Order?

A debtor who intends to make an individual voluntary arrangement ("**IVA**") proposal who meets the criteria under s.253(3) may apply for an interim order under s.253. An interim order has the effect that *inter alia* no bankruptcy petition against the debtor can be presented or proceeded with. An interim order is sought where the debtor seeks the protection of the moratorium provided by s.252 so that creditors in due course may consider the proposal.

The proposal itself is required to form part of the evidence in support of such an application.[137]

When the court is faced with a pending petition and an application for an interim order, the approach it will adopt is as follows.

By s.255 IA:

> (1) "The court shall not make an interim order on an application under section 253 unless it is satisfied—
>
> > (a) that the debtor intends to make a proposal under this Part;
> >
> > (b) that on the day of the making of the application the debtor was an undischarged bankrupt or was able to make a bankruptcy application;

[137] R.8.4 IR.

(c) that no previous application has been made by the debtor for an interim order in the period of 12 months ending with that day; and

(d) that the nominee under the debtor's proposal is willing to act in relation to the proposal.

(2) The court may make an order if it thinks that it would be appropriate to do so for the purpose of facilitating the consideration and implementation of the debtor's proposal."

As regards s.255(2) the court has a very wide discretion to determine whether an interim order should be made. The test is that the court must be satisfied that a debtor's proposal is serious and viable.[138]

It is a relevant factor whether a debtor has made a full and correct disclosure of his affairs.[139]

In *Hook v Jewson Ltd*[140] Sir Richard Scott, V-C. issued the following guidance:

> *"Judges must, I think, be careful not to allow applications for interim orders simply to become a means of postponing the making of bankruptcy orders in circumstances where there is no apparent likelihood of benefit to the creditors from such postponement."*

Equally, the court can take into account wider litigation conduct issues in relation to disclosure of financial affairs:

---

138 Davidson v Stanley [2004] EWHC 2595 (Ch);[2005] BPIR 279 [21-22].

139 [2004] EWHC 2595 (Ch); [2005] BPIR 279 [22].

140 [1997] 1 BCLC 664 at 668; [1997] B.P.I.R 100.

> "*[43] There are other factors which weigh with me in coming to this conclusion. As my recital of the background events makes clear, Mr Davidson, unfortunately, is somebody who has persistently failed in other proceedings, and despite orders of the court, to make full and frank disclosure of his financial affairs. Such conduct, as it seems to me, augurs badly for the success of a proposal of this nature. Moreover, Mr Davidson has been found in those other proceedings to be dishonest and indifferent to his obligations to the courts. I also have a strong sense that part of the motivation for this proposal is to delay the making of a bankruptcy order and possibly also to inhibit the further prosecution of the proceedings currently being brought against him by Oystertec.*"[141]

The purpose of the discretion enjoyed by the court is to act as a filter to avoid the unnecessary and wasteful convening of creditor's meetings if the proposal is one which is neither serious nor viable.[142]

As to the serious and viable test:

(1) "*For an IVA proposal to be serious it is not sufficient that it is seriously made or that it is made bona fide, it must have substance and is one which should seriously be considered by the creditors or be capable of serious consideration. It should not be derisory*".[143]

(2) There is no need to show that the proposal will survive any challenge and will be approved. The court is not permitted to pre-empt the decision of the creditors by deciding that a proposal is inadequate and therefore not serious. Equally,

---

141 [2004] EWHC 2595 (Ch); [2005] BPIR 279 [43]

142 Tucker v Atkins [2014] EWHC 2260 (Ch); [2014] B.P.I.R 1569 [32-33].

143 Shah v Cooper and Another [2003] BPIR 1018 [67]

> not everything is left to creditors and the court's role is to determine whether the proposal is fit to be put to the creditors; if so, it is for the creditors to determine whether the proposal is acceptable or not.[144]

That is not to say, however, that the court is powerless; courts have held that proposals have failed to meet to the serious and viability tests when they have amounted to an 'essay in make believe'.[145]

It may be the case that the petitioning creditor is able to assert that their debt is of sufficient amount to block the proposal from attaining sufficient majority to be passed, see r.15.34 IR. There is authority to the effect that in such circumstances a court is entitled to refuse an application under s.253 where it is 'strongly improbable' or clear that the proposal would not be approved.[146] The difficulty with such an approach however, is that there may not be before the court a definitive list of creditors which of course would inhibit such an argument from being made.

The Debt Respite Scheme (Breathing Space Moratorium and Mental Health Crisis Moratorium) (England and Wales) Regulations 2020[147]

Moratoriums & Duration

Two forms of moratoria are available under the Regulations. They are:

---

[144] [2003] BPIR 1018 [75-77]

[145] [2004] EWHC 2595 (Ch [2005] BPIR 279 at [42] Re Babaee [2024] EWHC 444 (Ch); [2024] B.P.I.R. 527 [112]

[146] Singh v Singh [2014] BPIR 1555 at [12] [16] and [22]; Tucker v Atkins [2014] EWHC 2260 (Ch) [32-33].

[147] Hereafter referred to as the Regulations.

(i) a breathing space moratorium and (ii) a mental health crisis moratorium.

The duration of a mental health crisis moratorium is set out in Regulation 32:

> "32.—(1) A mental health crisis moratorium starts on the day following the day on which the Secretary of State causes an entry to be made on the register in accordance with regulation 31(2)(a).
>
> (2) A mental health crisis moratorium ends on the earliest of—
>
> (a) the end of the period of 30 days beginning with the day on which the debtor stops receiving mental health crisis treatment,
>
> (b) the end of the period of 30 days beginning with the day on which a debt advice provider makes a request to the debtor's nominated point of contact in accordance with regulation 33 and during which period the debt advice provider does not receive a response,
>
> (c) the day on which cancellation of the mental health crisis moratorium takes effect under regulations 18, 19 or 34, or
>
> (d) the day on which it ends in accordance with regulation 21 as a result of the death of the debtor."

The duration of a breathing space moratorium is set out in Regulation 26:

> "26.—(1) A breathing space moratorium starts on the day following the day on which the Secretary of State causes an

> entry to be made on the register in accordance with regulation 25(2)(a).
>
> (2) A moratorium continues for 60 days beginning with the date on which it started in accordance with paragraph (1) unless—
>
> (a) it ends in accordance with regulation 21 as a result of the death of the debtor, or
>
> (b) it is cancelled in accordance with regulations 18, 19 or 27.

Effect of Moratorium

A creditor is prevented from presenting a bankruptcy petition against a debtor in relation to a moratorium debt during a moratorium period[148]. Unless, however, the court gives permission for the creditor to take that step. There are no reported cases as far as the authors are aware where the court has considered whether permission should be granted. In the authors' view, the likely factor the court will have regard to is the likelihood of the debtor being able to settle the petition debt or otherwise avoid a bankruptcy order from being made.

Equally, where a party has entered a moratorium and there is an extant petition, then the creditor and the court are subject to the following obligations:

> "**10.**—(1) If at the start of a moratorium a creditor to whom a moratorium debt is owed has a bankruptcy petition or any other action or other proceeding in any court or tribunal

[148] R.7 of the Regulations.

> pending in relation to a moratorium debt, then the creditor must notify the court or tribunal of the moratorium.
>
> (2) After a court or tribunal has received a notification referred to in paragraph (1) or is otherwise made aware of a moratorium—
>
> (a) any bankruptcy petition in relation to a moratorium debt must be stayed by the court until the moratorium ends or is cancelled, and
>
> (b) the court or tribunal must deal with any other action or proceeding in relation to a moratorium debt in accordance with this regulation."

Regulation 10, however, is expressed to be subject to Regulation 7(2)(b) by virtue of regulation 10(8) such that the court has the power to allow the bankruptcy petition to proceed as Zacaroli J (as he then was) explained in *Carter v Davies*[149]

> *"If Regulation 10(2)(b) had been intended to relate only to regulation 10(5), then it might be expected to have said that. In my view, the better interpretation is that the cross-reference to Regulation 7(2)(b) is intended to make any part of Regulation 10 which prohibits a creditor pursuing proceedings subject to the power of the court (derived from Regulation 7(2)(b)) to give permission to the contrary. The purpose of Regulation 7(2)(b) is to ensure the court retains control over proceedings before it. I see no purpose in prohibiting the court from retaining such control in respect of a bankruptcy petition. Indeed, for reasons I develop below, I consider that there are reasons to interpret the*

[149] [2024] EWHC 1536 (Ch); [2024] B.P.I.R. 934 [69]

> *Regulations as ensuring that the bankruptcy court does retain control in respect of a pending bankruptcy petition.*

In practice, this may be unlikely to occur – the court will be more likely to give effect to the moratorium in light of the underlying policy reasons surrounding its introduction. That being said, in *Yianni v Paliouras*[150] ICC Judge Mullen allowed a petition to proceed notwithstanding the existence of a breathing space moratorium because he was satisfied that: (i) the breathing space moratorium was being used tactically and (ii) given that the purpose of the legislation is to provide a debtor with protection so that they can take advice or enter sustainable debt solutions, in this case, the debtor had ample opportunity to take advice or enter sustainable debt solutions.

In addition to what is said above, in the authors' view, additional factors to which the court may be likely to have regard are: (i) the likelihood of the debtor being able to settle the petition debt or otherwise avoid a bankruptcy order being made; (ii) whether there is evidence of asset dissipation.

Regulation 7(12) provides that "Any action taken contrary to this regulation shall be null and void". However, this does not apply to a bankruptcy order which is obtained contrary to regulation 10(2)(a), as was held in *Carter v Davies* where a bankruptcy order had been made in circumstances where the court was unaware that a moratorium had been entered.

However, it does follow that a party who presents a petition without having obtained the court's permission to take that step will fall foul of regulation 7(12) and will therefore be automatically null and void. Indeed, the wording of regulation 7(2)(a) and (b) indicates that permission needs to be obtained *prior* to the relevant step being taken.

---

150 [2024] EWHC 1301 (Ch); [2024] B.P.I.R. 1420

Pending Application?

For the purposes of a mental health crisis moratorium, the Regulations envision an application made by prescribed persons in Regulation 29 which is supported by evidence of an approved mental health professional that the relevant debtor is receiving mental health crisis treatment. Pursuant to Regulation 32, the moratorium begins when the Secretary of State causes an entry to be made on the register in accordance with Regulation 31(2)(a). The Secretary of State will also notify the debtor's nominated point of contact and the relevant creditors of the start of the mental health crisis moratorium.

However, it may be that an application for a moratorium has been made but has not yet been determined by the time of the hearing of the bankruptcy petition. The court has jurisdiction to make a bankruptcy order as no moratorium would be in force in those circumstances (and even if there was, the court as above would still have jurisdiction to make a bankruptcy order if it granted permission for the petitioner to continue with the petition).

In the author's experience, a court is more likely to adjourn pending the outcome of the application for a mental health crisis moratorium (assuming there is nothing obviously defective about the application, for instance no evidence in support from an approved mental health professional). This is because it would certainly be a pyrrhic victory if after making a bankruptcy order the application for the moratorium was then granted and of course the making of a bankruptcy order in such circumstances would defeat the purpose of the moratorium application.

However, a word of caution is necessary here – the court's patience is not unlimited, and it will expect a full explanation by way of evidence if matters have not moved on by the time of the adjourned hearing. Practitioners would do well to demonstrate that they are taking every step in ensuring the matter is progressed as quickly as possible by liaising with the relevant debt advice provider.

CHAPTER FIVE

INCAPACITY

Issues of capacity can and do arise in bankruptcy petitions. In this chapter, we will consider the position of either a debtor or petitioner who appears to lack capacity within the meaning of the Mental Capacity Act 2005 or suffers from a physical affliction or disability. We will then consider how the court approaches these sorts of issues.

Importance of Capacity

In *Masterman-Lister v. Brutton & Co*[151] it was held that:

> *"Mr Francis submits, and I accept, that this is a matter which should be considered by the Rules Committee, and meanwhile courts should always, as a matter of practice, at the first convenient opportunity, investigate the question of capacity whenever there is any reason to suspect that it may be absent (e.g. significant head injury) other than in cases where there has already been an order pursuant to section 94(2) of the 1983 Act."*

That dictum applies equally in insolvency cases.

The Rules

The provisions of r.12.23-12.26 apply, pursuant to r.12.23 when "it appears to the court in insolvency proceedings that a person affected by

[151] (2003) 1WLR 1511 [17]

the proceedings is unable to manage and administer that person's own property and affairs by reason of (i) lacking capacity within the meaning of the Mental Capacity Act 2005; (ii) suffering from a physical affliction; or (iii) disability."[152]

These are disjunctive conditions and are more extensive than the categories of persons called 'protected parties' under the CPR because the Insolvency Rules also covers those with a physical affliction or disability.[153]

When the conditions under r.12.23 are engaged, by r.12.24 "the court may appoint such person as it thinks just to appear for, represent or act for the incapacitated person". Again, by that provision, the court may make that appointment either of its own motion or upon an application by:

- "a person who has been appointed by a court in the United Kingdom or elsewhere to manage the affairs of, or to represent, the incapacitated person;
- any person who appears to the court to be a suitable person to make the application;
- the official receiver; or
- the office-holder."

That application may be made without notice, although the court may require notice to be given to any other person (including the

[152] R.12.23 IR

[153] [64].

incapacitated person) and may adjourn the hearing of the application to enable that notice to be given.[154]

A witness statement made by a registered medical practitioner as to the physical or mental condition of the incapacitated person must be provided in support of the application.[155]

The court, on hearing the application may appoint a person for the purpose of a particular application or proceeding or indeed more generally. It may equally appoint the person for the purpose of exercising rights or powers which the incapacitated person might have exercised but for their incapacity.[156]

Relationship with CPR & Approach Taken by The Court

It has been said that the provisions of the CPR sit alongside the Insolvency Rules with the latter supplementing the former in insolvency cases.[157]

In this regard, where the court appoints a person under r.12.23 IR, it may well give permission within CPR r.21.3(2) or (3) for steps to be taken without appointing a litigation friend. The court has described such a course as 'obviously likely and sensible no doubt in many cases' but both provisions, i.e r.12.23 and CPR r.21.3 both have to be considered in an insolvency case.[158]

---

[154] R.12.24 (4) (5)

[155] R.12.25 IR.

[156] R.12.24 (2)

[157] [2011] EWHC 3809 (Ch); [2012] B.P.I.R. 793 [64]

[158] [2012] B.P.I.R. 793 [66]

It will normally be unnecessary and wasteful for the court to appoint a person under both the Insolvency Rules and the CPR, but the court must consider all powers available to it.[159]

In a case where it is clear that a bankruptcy order should be made and that there is nothing which a litigation friend or a person appointed under the IR could say to resist the making of such an order, then it is open to the court to proceed without appointing a person. That will be on the basis that it will be unjust for the hearing to be adjourned in order to allow for a person to be appointed. Vos J (as he then was) gave an example (and in the authors' view, it remains just that: only an example rather than being an exhaustive rule) of the above:

> *"70. It is there that, in my judgment, the Registrar was mistaken in this particular case. I do not say that she would have been mistaken in every case. If, for example, there had been clear evidence before the Registrar that (a) the debtor owed a particular sum of money, and that (b) the debtor had no assets, and that (c) the debtor had serious substantial liabilities so that nothing could possibly have been said by a litigation friend or by a representative appointed under Rule 7.44 that would change the position, it would have been open to the Registrar to decide that it would have been unreasonable and unjust to the petitioning creditor to adjourn the matter for the litigation friend or a deputy or a representative to be appointed."*[160]

However, in cases where that is not so, the court must consider whether a person should be appointed rather than proceeding to make a bankruptcy order.[161]

---

159 [2011] EWHC 3809 (Ch) [2012] B.P.I.R. 793 [66]

160 [2012] B.P.I.R. 793 [70]

161 [2011] EWHC 3809 (Ch) [2012] B.P.I.R. 793 [70]

In practice, however, it is extremely unlikely that a court would conclude that there would be nothing that an appointed person could possibly say and proceed to make a bankruptcy order. On the contrary, the court is much more likely to err on the side of caution and either appoint a person or adjourn for the purposes of enabling an appointment to be made.

CHAPTER SIX

INSOLVENT ADMINISTRATION ORDERS

The primary piece of legislation concerning the law of insolvency and deceased persons is the Administration of Insolvent Estates of Deceased Persons Order 1986.[162]

There are a couple of relevant scenarios. The first, of course, is when an individual dies insolvent. The second is where an individual dies after a bankruptcy petition is presented but before a bankruptcy order is made. We discuss these, along with other relevant aspects below.

(a) Legislative Overview

The DPO modifies various sections of the Act. The provisions of the Act which are set out in the DPO will apply, along with the IR. In the event of a conflict between the IR and the DPO, the latter will apply.

(b) Individual Dies Insolvent

The DPO retains s.264 albeit in an amended form which allows a creditor or a personal representative to present a petition for an insolvent administration order against an individual.

But first, by s.271(2) of the Act as amended by the DPO:

[162] Hereafter referred to as the DPO.

> "A petition for an insolvency administration order shall not be presented to the court after proceedings have been commenced in any court of justice for the administration of the deceased debtor's estate."

Assuming the above is not engaged, s.267(2) of the Act is modified so that it in this context it reads as follows:

> "(a) the amount of the debt, or the aggregate amount of the debts, owed by the debtor would have been equal to or exceeded the bankruptcy level, or
>
> (b) the debt, or each of the debts, owed by the debtor would have been for a liquidated sum payable to the petitioning creditor, or one or more of the petitioning creditors, either immediately or at some certain future time, and would have been unsecured.".

It has been suggested that the reference to 'or' is an error and that both conditions must be satisfied[163].

The court has a discretion over whether to make an insolvent administration order. Under s.271 of the Act as modified by the DPO (insofar as relevant) and when the petition is brought by anyone other than a personal representative it is provided:

> "Section 271 as if for that section there were substituted the following:—
>
> (1) The court may make an insolvency administration order on a petition for such an order under section 264(1) if it is satisfied —

[163] *Watson & Baister: Bankruptcy: Law And Practice* [20.010]

(a) that the debt, or one of the debts, in respect of which the petition was presented is a debt which,

(i) having been payable at the date of the petition or having since become payable, has neither been paid nor secured or compounded for; or

(ii) has no reasonable prospect of being able to be paid when it falls due; and

(b) that there is a reasonable probability that the estate will be insolvent."

In practice, these sorts of petitions are usually one sided and have been brought by arm's length creditors. That creditor will not have access to the estate's books and records and the court will usually be willing to infer that the reason why payment has not been made is because the estate is unable to pay.

In circumstances where the matter is not one sided and a party is properly representing the estate of the deceased, they may well be able to point to documentation which shows that the estate is not in fact insolvent and can meet the petition debt in full. This is markedly different from the position which would apply if the debtor had been alive, where assertion of solvency is no answer if the petition debt has not been paid.[164]

Conversely, when the petition is presented by a personal representative that can only be on the grounds that the estate is insolvent and they must also produce a statement of affairs detailing the deceased debtor's assets and liabilities etc.

---

[164] Johnson v Tandridge District Council [2007] EWHC 3325 (Ch); 2008] B.P.I.R. 405 [37].

(c) Death After Presentation of Petition

In *Domenico Berti v Steele Raymond (A Firm)*[165] the Court of Appeal neatly summarised the position where: (i) a debtor dies after presentation but before service of the petition and (ii) where a debtor dies after presentation and service of the petition. In both scenarios the Petition has not yet been finally heard.

> *"The Administration of Insolvent Estates of Deceased Persons Order 1986 ("the Administration Order") was made under section 421. Article 5 provides as follows:*
>
> *"(1) If a debtor, by or against whom a bankruptcy petition has been presented, dies, the proceedings in the matter shall, unless the court otherwise orders, be continued as if he were alive, with the modifications specified in Schedule 2 of this order.*
>
> *(2) The reasonable funeral and testamentary expenses have priority over the preferential debts listed in Schedule 6 to the Act.*
>
> *(3) If a debtor dies after presentation of a bankruptcy petition but before service the court may order service to be effected on his personal representative or other person as it thinks fit".*
>
> *4. The modifications in Schedule 2 are not relevant here. Article 5(3) is also reproduced, almost word for word, in rule 6.16 of the Insolvency Rules 1986 . These provisions do not in terms apply where a debtor dies after the service of the petition but before the petition has been heard, but rule 7.51 of the Insolvency Rules , as substituted by the Insolvency (Amendment) (No 2) Rules 1999 , provides for the Civil Procedure Rules and any relevant Practice Directions to apply in any insolvency*

165 [2001] EWCA Civ 2079; [2002] B.P.I.R. 683

proceedings with any modifications, unless that would be inconsistent with the Insolvency Rules themselves. That lets in the general provisions in rule 19.8 of the Civil Procedure Rules as to the death of a party. Paragraph (1) is in the following terms:

"Where a person who has an interest in a claim has died and that person has no personal representative, the court may order —

(a) the claim to proceed in the absence of a person representing the estate of the deceased, or

(b) a person to be appointed to represent the estate of the deceased."

5.. I will not read the other paragraphs of rule 19.8, but it is apparent from the rule as a whole that it gives the court quite wide powers to dispense with the need for a formal grant of probate or letters of administration after the death of a party. It seems to recognise that, especially with relatively small claims, the need for a formal grant may be disproportionate and cause unnecessary delay and expense."

CHAPTER SEVEN

PROCEDURE

The procedural rules which govern a creditor's bankruptcy petition are contained in Part 10 of the IR and the PDIP.

Statutory Demand

The opening chapter of Part 10 IR deals with statutory demands.

By s. 268, in order to demonstrate that a debtor is unable to pay a debt, a creditor can either serve a statutory demand on the debtor (s. 268(1)(a)) or prove that execution or other process in respect of a debt on a judgment is returned unsatisfied in whole or in part (s. 268(1)(b)). In the authors' experience, the former is by far the most common way of proving inability to pay debts.

A statutory demand is not a document which needs to be issued by or presented to the court; it is a document that is completed by the creditor (or creditor's lawyers) and then served on the debtor. It is not a court document.

R. 10.1(1) IR sets out a lengthy and detailed list of matters that must be stated in the statutory demand. Those include the identification details of the debtor, the name and address of the creditor, and importantly a statement of the amount of the debt and the consideration for the debt. It is a good discipline for a creditor (or those advising it) to check that each of the matters specified in r. 10.1(1) IR is covered as appropriate to the relevant case. A template statutory demand appears as a weblink to paragraph 11.1 of the PDIP.

There are specific rules which apply where interest is claimed from the debtor: r. 10.1(7) IR, and where the creditor holds security in respect of the debt: r. 10.1(9) IR. In summary, the demand must set out the nature of the security and the value that the creditor places on it, and then the amount of the debt less the specified value of the security.

Once a demand has been completed, it must be dated and authenticated either by the creditor or by a person who is authorised to make the demand on the creditor's behalf (r. 10.1(5) IR).

The next step is service. The creditor is required to do "*all that is reasonable to bring the statutory demand to the debtor's attention*", which, if the circumstances allow, means personal service (r. 10.2 IR). The bar has been described as a '*high one*'[166]. Of course, each case will turn on its own facts, but if, for example, a creditor is aware of both a personal residence and a business address for the debtor, attempts should be made to serve at both if an initial at service at one is unsuccessful.

The provisions on service in the IR are supplemented by the PDIP (paragraphs 11.2 and 11.3). Where personal service is not possible, doing everything that is reasonable to bring the demand to the debtor's attention could include the steps necessary to justify an order for substituted service of a bankruptcy petition (they are set out in paragraph 12.7 PDIP) or any other form communication, whether physical or electronic.

The steps in paragraph 12.7 include one personal call at the debtor's personal residence and place of business (assuming a debtor has both). If that doesn't achieve personal service, then a letter should be written referring to the unsuccessful attendance(s) and giving (at least two business days) notice of a future attendance. The letter can be posted by mail, or by inserting into a letterbox. The letter should of course contain

[166] Regional Collection Services Ltd v Heald [2000] B.P.I.R. 661; Bush v Bank Mandiri (Europe) Ltd [2011] B.P.I.R. 19.

contact details and invite the debtor to make alternative arrangements for personal service if the proposed future attendance is not convenient. It should also contain a warning that if the debtor is not present for the attendance, then the creditor will serve the statutory demand by either advertisement, post or by insertion in a letter box.

In the authors' experience, service of a statutory demand (as with service of a bankruptcy petition) is normally undertaken by a specialist process server, on the instructions of the creditor. It is rare, but not unheard of, for there to be disputes over whether valid service of a statutory demand has taken place.

A failure to serve a statutory demand can lead to the dismissal of a subsequently presented bankruptcy petition based on that demand.[167]

Where there has been a fundamental failure to effect service, that is to say, for instance, when the statutory demand never reached the debtor or came within his dominion due to a failure to comply with the practice direction/ r.10.2 then there is no scope for r.12.64 to remedy the defect.[168]

Whereas, if a statutory demand has ultimately reached a debtor or where at least some steps have been taken in compliance with the practice direction, then there is scope for the application of r.12.64. As the court suggested in *Clauson v Knowles Construction Ltd:*[169]

---

167 Canning v Irwin Mitchell LLP [2017] EWHC 718 (Ch); [2017] BPIR 934 [29-30]. This can be contrasted with a situation where, even though the demand may not have come to the debtor's notice, the creditor has still done all that is reasonable to serve the demand: Emmanuel v Commissioners for HMRC [2017] EWHC 1253 (Ch); [2017] B.P.I.R. 1182 [35-36].

168 Canning v Irwin Mitchell LLP [2017] EWHC 718 (Ch), [2017] BPIR 934

169 [2024] EWHC 1520 (Ch); [2024] B.P.I.R. 949

> "49.1. However, where service of a statutory demand is a jurisdictional pre-requisite of a bankruptcy petition and must (if the petition is not to be dismissed) either be achieved in strict conformity with rule 10.2 of the IR 2016 , or, if circumstances permit, achieved in sufficient conformity to allow for any irregularity or defect to be cured under rule 12.64;
>
> 49.2. a statutory demand is in principle capable of being set aside under rule 10.5(5)(d), although under rule 10.5, the court has a discretion and has powers, which are capable of meeting or addressing certain issues of prejudice that might otherwise be suffered by a debtor.

In those circumstances they key questions will be ameliorating any prejudice that might have been caused; the practical reality is that at the petition stage, that would simply involve adjourning the petition to grant the debtor any time that he might have lost because of defective service.

In practice, the court is unlikely to spend much time debating whether there was a fundamental failure to serve or a partial failure. Save for the most egregious cases where no attempt is made at all to serve the debtor, the court will likely be guided by considerations of prejudice and proportionality. Particularly where the underlying debt is not disputed.

A statutory demand can be served outside the jurisdiction of England and Wales. The PDIP contains provisions in the event that the relevant country is party to an applicable civil procedure convention (paragraph 11.3 PDIP). If a demand is to be served outside of the jurisdiction, care must be taken to identify (and then state in the demand) the correct number of days for an application to set aside the demand (and the correct number of days after which a bankruptcy petition can be presented): r. 10.1(10) and the table in CPR PD6B.

Once at least 3 weeks have elapsed after service of the statutory demand in the jurisdiction (or the appropriate number of days in the case of a demand served out of the jurisdiction), and assuming that the demand has not been complied with nor set aside, the debtor is deemed to be unable to pay his debts (s. 268(1)(a)). That opens the door for the presentation of a bankruptcy petition.

To set aside a statutory demand, the debtor must make a court application, supported by evidence. There is a strict time limit of 18 days (if the demand was served in the jurisdiction) after service of the demand to make the application (r. 10.4(2) IR). It is possible for the court to extend that time limit: s. 376. The court will take into account (and so evidence supporting an extension application ought to address) the substantive merits of the set aside application, the reason for failing to comply with the deadline, and any prejudice caused to either side if time is (/ is not) extended.[170] The evidence must also deal with whether the creditor has presented a petition. An application for relief from sanctions is not necessary,[171] although that doesn't mean that the normal CPR r. 3.9 criteria can just be ignored.[172] Paragraphs 11.4.2 and 11.4.3 of the PDIP also set out further practical matters which a debtor's advisors need to bear in mind (for example, the steps that need to be taken to lodge the application at court).

The evidence supporting the application must identify the date on which the debtor became aware of the demand, and the grounds on which the debtor relies to set it aside (r. 10.4(6) IR). Although of course the evidence should be as full and detailed as possible, in the authors' experience, the reality of having to prepare such evidence under the pressure of time (and usually prior to any form of serious disclosure having been given by the creditor) means that there are plenty of traps for the unwary in compiling the evidence. Evidence has to be given in witness statement form (supported by a statement of truth). If the

---

[170] Rankin v Dissington Lending Co Ltd [2021] EWHC 172 (Ch) [9].

[171] [2021] EWHC 172 (Ch) [8] [10].

[172] [2021] EWHC 172 (Ch) [10].

application succeeds, and the demand is set aside, it is, in the authors' experience, very common for the creditor to then issue CPR Part 7 proceedings. Statements made in hurriedly prepared evidence can and do sometimes come back to bite the debtor once full disclosure has taken place in any subsequent Part 7 claim.

Once the application is received by the court, it will list a hearing giving the parties at least five business days' notice (r. 10.5(3) IR)[173]. That first hearing is usually only given a short time estimate and is normally used for the purposes of giving directions on the application. In rarer cases, the court might be persuaded to reach a final determination on the application, even if the hearing has such a short listing. The directions normally provide for the creditor to file responsive evidence, for the debtor to file reply evidence and then for the listing of a hearing to determine the substantive issues that arise on the application; the length of that hearing is normally measured in hours (anything longer is strongly suggestive of the fact that any dispute is not capable of resolution at the statutory demand stage).

Setting Aside a Demand

From the perspective of a debtor, there is strategic merit in applying to set aside a statutory demand: it will delay the presentation of a petition. Once a petition is presented, the debtor becomes subject to s. 284 (void dispositions) and it is also the date from which the 'lookback' period starts for the purposes of transaction avoidance (s. 341). Creditors and their advisors are of course alive to this, and when acting for the creditor,

[173] The IR allow for the possibility of the court dismissing an application on receipt if no cause is shown: r. 10.5(1). In the authors' experience this is a very rare occurrence, particularly in cases where the debtor is professionally advised.

it is important to ensure that the debtor doesn't unnecessarily delay the hearing of an application to set aside a demand.

The grounds on which the court may grant an application to set aside a demand are set out in r. 10.5(5). They are (a) if the debtor has a counterclaim, set-off or cross demand which equals or exceeds the amount of the debt, (b) the debt is disputed on grounds which appear to the court to be substantial, (c) the creditor has security and either r. 10.1(9) is not complied with or the value of the security exceeds the amount of the debt, or (d) on other grounds, the demand ought to be set aside. In practice, the most common grounds encountered on such applications are grounds (a), (b) and (d). There is a considerable amount of case law which addresses each ground, although it is fair to say that many first instance decisions are no more than examples of application of the principles to a specific set of facts. Each ground is considered in turn below.

The bar for a debtor seeking to set aside a statutory demand is relatively low. The court must be satisfied that there is a genuine triable issue. This has been likened to the real prospects of success test that applies in summary judgment applications under Part 24 of the CPR[174]. Further, parties should not lose sight of the fact that, on the hearing of an application to set aside a statutory demand, the lens through which the court is approaching matter is narrow: it is whether there is a debt (or, in the case of (a), a cross claim). This is not the same as the court deciding whether to make a bankruptcy order.

In determining whether to set aside a statutory demand, the court should not, and in the authors' experience, does not conduct a mini trial. The application is decided on the witness statements; in the vast majority of

[174] Ashworth v Newnote [2007] EWCA Civ 793, [2007] BPIR 1012 at [33], Collier v P & MJ Wright (Holdings) Ltd [2007] EWCA Civ 1329, [2008] 1 WLR 643 and Servis-Terminal LLC v Drelle [2023] EWHC 506 (Ch) [2024] BPIR 285 [7] [134].

cases, there is no cross-examination. This does not mean that a court must simply accept what is stated in a witness statement: "... *it would be open to the court to reject that evidence if it were inherently implausible or if it were contradicted, or were not supported, by contemporaneous documentation*".[175]

Cross Claims

The first ground, in r. 10.5(5)(a) is that the debtor can demonstrate a counterclaim, set-off or cross demand which equals or exceeds the debt claimed in the demand. There is a mutuality requirement between the two liabilities: the liability must be owed by / due to the debtor (or creditor, as appropriate) in the same legal capacity.[176] For example, if the debtor was sued in a capacity as a beneficiary of a trust but had a cross-demand in a capacity as a trustee, that mutuality requirement would not be met. The wording of 10.5(5)(a) is wide, including counterclaim, set-off or a cross demand; in view of that, a debtor does not have to bring themselves with the strict rules of legal or equitable set-off,[177] it does not matter that the two liabilities arise out of different transactions. Moreover, a contractual restriction (for example, an obligation to pay without set-off, or a pay now sue later clause) will not prevent a debtor relying on ground (a).[178] The debtor must, however, demonstrate that the value of their claims exceeds the value of the liability stated in the demand, even in a case where the difference is less than the bankruptcy

---

[175] Collier. There are similar statements in Ashworth: [34].

[176] Hurst v Bennett [2001] EWCA Civ 182; [2001] BPIR 287.

[177] King v Bar Mutual Indemnity Fund [2023] EWHC 1408 (Ch); [2023] B.P.I.R. 1386.

[178] Garrow v Society of Lloyd's [1999] BPIR 885.

level, the court would not set aside the demand in reliance on ground (a).[179]

Disputed debts

The second ground is that the debt is disputed on grounds which appear to the court to be substantial. This is the same in scope as challenging a bankruptcy petition on the grounds that the petition debt is disputed, and reference should be made to Chapter 3. The fact that the demand mistakenly overstates the debt does not translate into a finding that the whole debt is disputed.[180]

Specifically in relation to disputed debts, there is one important point of distinction between the position on the hearing of an application to set aside a statutory demand and the hearing of a bankruptcy petition. The PDIP provides that where the debt in the demand is based on a judgment, or an order, or a liability order, or a costs certificate, or a tax assessment or the decision of a tribunal, then the court will not inquire into the validity of the debt. Moreover, the court will also generally not adjourn the hearing pending an appeal or some other application to set aside the underlying document which creates the liability: paragraph 11.4.4.

Security

If the creditor that has served the statutory demand is fully secured because they hold security over the debtor's assets, then r. 10.5(5)(c) enables the debtor to obtain an order setting aside the demand. 'Security', for these purposes, is defined in s. 383. Where a creditor has security over a third party's assets, that does not fall within the definition of s. 383,

---

[179] Howell v Lerwick Commercial Mortgage Corp Ltd [2015] EWHC 1177 (Ch), [2015] 1 WLR 3554.

[180] In Re a Debtor (No 490/SD/91) [1993] BCLC 164.

and in that scenario, a debtor is not able to get the demand set aside relying on this ground.[181]

In some cases, there will be a dispute over the value of the security. In such a case, it is the debtor that must prove that the creditor is fully secured. This will need to be done by obtaining valuation evidence: the valuation basis would be on a forced sale basis.[182]

Other grounds

The relevant rule – r. 10.5(5)(d) – simply refers to the court being satisfied "on other grounds" that the statutory demand ought to be set aside. At first blush, this rule is very wide. Unsurprisingly, it has been circumscribed by case law, although (again unsurprisingly), judges are careful to make clear that new circumstances may arise in which r. 10.5(5)(d) can be deployed.

The grounds relied upon must have some relationship to the debt and the circumstances in which the debt has arisen.[183] In Jones v the Sky Wheels Group Ltd[184]Snowden J (as he then was), set out the most recent modern analysis of the provision. Clearly, as he said, "*it cannot be the case that the court has an unlimited freedom to take its own view of what is just and unjust. There must be recourse to some relevant legal principles....*" He endorsed the view that it was necessary to show a substantial reason, comparable to the sort of reasons available under grounds (a), (b) and (c).

181 Promontoria (Chestnut) Ltd v Bell [2019] EWHC 1581 (Ch) [2019] BPIR 1241 [26]-[28]

182 Platts v Western Trust & Savings Ltd [1996] BPIR 339. The costs of enforcing the security are not taken into account: Owo-Samson v Barclays Bank [2003] EWCA Civ 714; [2003] B.P.I.R. 1373

183 Turner v Turner [2006] EWHC 2023 (Ch), [2006] BPIR 1531.

184 [2020] EWHC 1112 (Ch); [2020] B.P.I.R. 851 [87]

By way of example, debtors have succeeded on ground (d) by arguing: that the demand caused genuine prejudice to the debtor because it was confusing,[185] or where it would have been illegal to pay the demand,[186] or if the debtor is a guarantor, and the creditor was prevented from proceeding against the principal,[187] or the liability under the guarantee hasn't been triggered,[188] or where the demand is for an amount only marginally above the bankruptcy level and the debtor has offered to pay enough to reduce it below the bankruptcy level, meaning that a petition would likely fail,[189] or where it is an abuse of process or the creditor is acting for a collateral purpose.[190]

By contrast, a debtor who wishes to argue that the court would not have jurisdiction over them in the event that a bankruptcy petition were presented cannot rely on r. 10.5(5)(d); rather, it is necessary to apply for an antisuit injunction (potentially coupled with an application to set aside the demand).[191] Trivial mistakes in a demand will also not give rise to an order setting aside the demand.[192]

---

185 Re a Debtor (No 1 of 1987) [1989] 1 WLR 271.

186 Libyan Investment Authority v Maud [2016] EWCA Civ 788.

187 John Remblance v Octagon Assets Ltd [2009] EWCA Civ 581; [2009] B.P.I.R. 1129

188 Martin v Mclaren Construction Ltd [2019] EWHC 2059 (Ch); [2019] B.P.I.R. 1506.

189 City Electrical Factors Ltd v Hardingham [1996] BPIR 541.

190 Maud v Aabar Block Sarl and Edgeworth Capital (Luxembourg) Sarl [2015] EWHC 1626 (Ch), [2015] BPIR 845 and Johnson v Desiman Ltd [2024] 3 WLUK 727.

191 Pérétie v Eden Farm [2025] EWHC 1349 (Ch); [2025] B.P.I.R. 985

192 Agilo Ltd v Henry [2010] EWHC 2717 (Ch); [2011] B.P.I.R. 297

Following the application

If the application is successful, that is the end of the insolvency road for the particular creditor in respect of the debts claimed in the demand.

By contrast, if the application is unsuccessful, the insolvency process continues in earnest. By r. 10.5(8) IR, on dismissal of an application, the court must make an order authorising the creditor to present a bankruptcy petition either as soon as reasonably practicable, or after a date specifically identified in the order.

The date of presentation of a petition is often a point of dispute after the court's judgment on the substance of the application has been delivered. The order normally sought by the creditor is that presentation of the petition should be permitted to take place forthwith (not only does the creditor wished to be paid as soon as possible, but the sooner the petition is presented, the sooner the look back period starts for avoidance transactions (s 341)); the debtor may wish to argue that some time should be allowed before the petition is presented. One basis for obtaining more time is if the debtor wishes to pay the debt or try to arrive at some compromise with the creditor.[193]

The legal costs of an application to set aside a statutory demand normally follow the event in accordance with standard CPR costs principles.

[193] Davies v Barnes Webster & Sons Ltd [2011] EWHC 2560 (Ch); [2012] B.P.I.R. 97 (albeit that was an unusual case involving the president and one of the trustees of an unincorporated association who, having failed to set aside a statutory demand needed time to arrange payment of the debt relying on his indemnity from the association) at [44] and Darbyshire v Turpin [2013] EWHC 954 (Ch); [2013] B.P.I.R. 558 [19].

Of course, arguments which were unsuccessfully deployed by a debtor at the statutory demand stage cannot be run again on the hearing of the petition; the debtor does not get two bites at the cherry.[194]

It is in the creditor's interest to get on and present the petition as soon as possible after any application to set aside the statutory demand is set aside: that is because the effect of r. 10.7(2), is that if there is a delay longer than 4 months between the demand and the petition, the same must be explained in the petition. In practice, a delay of slightly longer than 4 months is not a bar to the presentation of a petition, particularly where the delay is attributable to having to deal with an application to set aside a statutory demand. Of course, the longer the delay, the more likely a debtor will be able to argue that the demand is redundant or is no longer an accurate guide to the debtor's inability to pay his debts.

Presentation of the Petition

A petition must be filed with the court (r. 10.12).[195] The IR specify the number of copies of the petition which must be delivered; a creditor should check this: (r. 10.12(4)). On receipt, the court will endorse the petition with the date and time of filing, it will apply the court seal to it, and it will fix a venue for the first hearing of the petition (r. 10.12(5)-(7)). The creditor's lawyers must also produce a receipt of the deposit payable to the Official Receiver (r. 10.12(2)) and must pay the court fee

[194] Harvey Dunbar Assets plc [2015] EWHC 3355 (Ch); [2016] B.P.I.R. 48 Conversely, if there was no application to set aside the demand, or the debtor wishes to raise new points, that is permissible: Barnes v Whitehead [2004] BPIR 693.

[195] Depending whether the court uses a Courts Electronic Filing system (CE-file), the petition can either be CE-filed, or filed in hardcopy. CE-filing is currently compulsory in the Business and Property Courts nationwide.

(paragraphs 12.4.1 to 12.4.3 of the PDIP). The relevant court fees are specified in the Insolvency Proceedings (Fees) Order 2016.

As for contents, these are also prescribed by the IR: r. 10.7. There is no prescribed form for a creditor's bankruptcy petition. There are also detailed rules which govern the identification of the debtor and the debt (rr. 10.8 and 10.9 respectively). A creditor would be well-advised to check off that each of the matters referred to in those rules is appropriately (and where relevant) completed in the petition. The matters to be stated include identification of the jurisdictional anchor (see Chapter 3 for more information on jurisdiction), as well as more obvious details such as name, trading name, occupation, and address and contact details.

Pursuant to the PDIP, where the petition has been preceded by a statutory demand, only the debt claimed in the statutory demand can be claimed in the petition (paragraph 12.2.2).

In relation to the debt (or debts; a petition can be presented in respect of more than one debt), the amount of the debt and either the consideration for it, or a description of how the debt arose. There are particular provisions concerning charges by way of interest: r. 10.9(1)(b)-(e). It is also necessary to state that the debt is unsecured (r. 10.9(f)). A petition should not include interest that has accrued after the date of the statutory demand.[196]

In the case of a petition that was preceded by a statutory demand, the petition must specify the date and manner of service of the demand, and also that the demand hasn't been complied with and that no application to set aside the demand is outstanding: r. 10.9(2). The PDIP contains further requirements that must be complied with: paragraph 12.2.4.

196 Moorgate Industries UK Ltd v Mittal [2020] EWHC 1550 (Ch); [2020] B.P.I.R. 1151

In those rare cases where the petition is preceded not by a statutory demand, but by unsatisfied execution of a judgment, the petition must state the court which issued the execution or other process, giving particulars of the return: r. 10.9(3).

Once the creditor has completed the petition, it is necessary for the creditor (or a creditor's representative) to verify the petition by a statement of truth: r. 10.10(1).[197] Practice Direction 22 of the CPR sets out example statements of truth. The template bankruptcy petitions which are available on legal research and resource sites are normally pre-populated with a statement of truth. The statement of truth must be authenticated and dated by the person verifying it (r. 10.10(4)).

Prior to presenting the petition to court, the creditor must also conduct an Official Search with the Chief Land Registrar in the register of pending actions for pending petitions presented against the same debtor: paragraph 12.3.1 of the PDIP. The PDIP then imposes some boilerplate wording to be included in the petition. Again, the templates available on legal research and resource sites include the relevant wording (paragraph 12.2.3).

A creditor needs to ensure that a petition is presented to the right court. The rules are in r. 10.11. If the proceedings are allocated to the London Insolvency District, then if the debt is £50,000 or more, then the petition must be presented to the High Court (conversely if it is less than £50,000 it must be presented to the county Court at Central London): r. 10.11(1). The rule is currently supplemented by a Pilot Practice Note (revised): Listing and Criteria for Transfer of Work 2024. The effect of that practice note is that certain matters are transferred from the High Court

---

[197] If the petition includes different debts from different creditors, then each creditor must verify the petition: r. 10.10(2). Such petitions are comparatively rare.

to the County Court at Central London (paragraphs 6 and 7, which, in the case of bankruptcy petitions, sets the debt threshold at £500,000).

The London Insolvency District comprises the areas served by hearing centres at: Barnet, Bow, Brentford, the County Court at Central London, Clerkenwell and Shoreditch, Edmonton, Lambeth, Mayor's and City of London Court, Wandsworth, West London, and Willesden.[198]

Where a debtor is resident in England and Wales, and the proceedings aren't allocated to the London Insolvency District, then the petition must be presented to the debtor's own hearing centre, which is determined in accordance with r. 10.11(4). This, in turn, depends on whether the debtor has carried on business in England and Wales within the six months preceding the petition. If he has, then it is to the hearing centre for the insolvency district where the debtor carried on business; if he hasn't then the appropriate hearing centre is the one for the insolvency district where the debtor resided.[199]

There are separate rules in relation to debtors in respect of whom an Individual Voluntary Arrangement is in force: r. 10.11(6), and debtors that are not resident in England and Wales (r. 10.11(5)). In the case of the latter, and provided that the proceedings are not allocated to the London Insolvency District and that the debtor did at least reside or carry on business in England and Wales in the 6 months preceding presentation, then a creditor can present the petition either in the High Court or in the debtor's own hearing centre.

---

[198] The London Insolvency District (County Court at Central London) Order 2014 (SI 2014/818).

[199] The insolvency districts are fixed by an order which was itself promulgated pursuant to s. 374. The Gov.UK: Find A Court or Tribunal webpage enables a creditor to search by postcode for the appropriate court. A list of County Court hearing centres with insolvency jurisdiction is contained in Schedule 6 to the IR.

Once a petition is accepted by the court, it will then cause an application for registration of the petition in the register of pending actions to the Chief Land Registrar: r. 10.13.[200]

A petition can be amended at any time after presentation with the permission of the court: r. 10.16.

Service of the Petition

A petition must be served: r. 10.14. That must be done in accordance with Schedule 4 to the IR. In the case of a petition, it must be served by personal service.[201] Service must be verified by a certificate of service, the contents of which are specified in paragraph 6 of Schedule 4.

However, by paragraph 1(5) of Schedule 4, if, for any reason, it is impracticable to effect service – in the case of a bankruptcy petition – by personal service, then service can be effected in such other manner as the court directs.

The steps that are necessary to obtain an order for substituted services (which is obtained on an application, supported by a witness statement) are set out in paragraph 12.7 of the PDIP. This provides that, '*in most cases*', the following will suffice. One personal call at the debtor's personal residence and place of business (assuming a debtor has both). If that doesn't achieve personal service, then a letter should be written referring

[200] A petition is presented not when received by the court, but when the Official Receiver's deposit is paid: Re a Company [2024] EWCA Civ 1436; [2025] B.P.I.R. 258

[201] Personal service includes, of course, handing it to the debtor, but in the case of a debtor refusing to accept a document, it is sufficient if the debtor knows that the document was a bankruptcy petition and the document was left near him: Gate Gourmet Luxembourg IV SARL v Morby [2016] EWHC 74 (Ch) [2016] BPIR 414 at [28] – [35].

to the unsuccessful attendance(s) and giving (at least two business days) notice of a future attendance. The letter can be posted by mail, or by inserting into a letterbox. The letter should of course contain contact details and invite the debtor to make alternative arrangements for personal service if the proposed future attendance is not convenient. It should also contain a warning that if the debtor is not present for the attendance, then the creditor will make an application to court for an order for substituted service.

The PDIP also specifies that, when the process server attends following a letter of appointment, they should make enquiries whether the debtor is still resident at the address, and if away, when they will return. If the debtor has lawyers acting for him, then the process server should of course attempt to arrange an appointment through those solicitors.

Normally, an application for permission to serve other than by personal service should be made before service by a different means is attempted. However, if the application is made after such service have been effected, the court retains the ability to waive the procedural irregularity using r. 12.64,[202] or it could potentially make a retroactive order for service.[203]

If, by the time that the creditor comes to serve the petition, the debtor is out of the jurisdiction, the creditor will need to apply for and obtain permission to serve the petition out of the jurisdiction. The grounds of jurisdiction are those set out in s. 265, albeit in deciding the application, the court would normally apply CPR Part 6 principles.[204]

---

202 Gate Gourmet Luxembourg IV SARL v Morby [2016] EWHC 74 (Ch) ; [2016] BPIR 414.

203 Ardawa v Uppal [2019] EWHC 465 (Ch); [2019] B.P.I.R. 475 but contrast Lau v Cowley [2020] EWHC 2429 (Ch); [2021] B.P.I.R. 312.

204 There is a discussion of the interaction between s. 26 and CPR Part 6 in Jones v Aston Risk Management Ltd [2024] EWHC 2553 (Ch); [2025] B.P.I.R. 280. Also, HRH Prince Hussam Bin Saud Bin Abdulaziz Al Saud

Once the creditor has received a sealed copy of the bankruptcy petition, it is important that they get on and serve it as soon as possible. This is because, by r. 10.21(1), the petition cannot be heard until at least 14 days have elapsed after service. In cases where less than 14 days have elapsed, the court is very likely to adjourn the hearing, with possible cost consequences for the creditor.[205] It is open to a creditor, before the date of the hearing, to ask the court to postpone the hearing pursuant to r. 10.22 – any such request will need to explain the late service (r. 10.22(2)), and moreover, the court may not allow the costs of the application (r. 10.22(3)).

Debtor's Notice of Opposition

Once a debtor has been served, they need to decide on how to respond, and whether they will oppose the making of a bankruptcy order.

A well-advised debtor will file a Notice of Opposition (r. 10.18). The rule is expressed in mandatory terms ("must"). The notice must be filed at court and delivered to the petitioning creditors not less than five business days before the hearing.

In practice, where a debtor complies with this rule, it is likely to mean that the first hearing of the petition will become a hearing for directions, rather than a substantive hearing of the petition.

---

v Mobile Telecommunications Co KSCP [2022] EWHC 744 (Ch); [2022] B.P.I.R. 1001.

[205] Where a debtor has absconded, or it is otherwise a proper case to do so – for example to protect assets- the court can hear the petition sooner than 14 days after service: r. 10.21(2).

Even where, as is common, a debtor doesn't comply with the rule, that is not usually fatal:[206] it is a frequent occurrence for debtors to attend at the first hearing without having filed any notice of objection, and to be granted the possibility (or, more usually, ordered to file the notice).

The Hearing

The petitioning creditor, the debtor, any IVA supervisor of the debtor, and any creditor that complies with r. 10.19 can appear at the hearing of the petition (r. 10.21(3)).

Any other creditor who becomes aware of the petition can – not later than 4pm on the business day before the hearing – give notice to the petitioning creditors whether they intend to appear and support or oppose the petition (r. 10.19), and indeed, the petitioning creditor must give the court, on the day of the hearing, a list of the persons intending to appear (r. 10.20(3). The IR specify the contents of the list. A supporting or opposing creditor who fails to give the relevant notice can only be heard with the permission of the court (r. 10.19(6)); in practice, it is very rare for such creditors not to be given permission to appear.

In addition to the list of creditors, the petitioning creditor must also come armed with a certificate of continuing debt to be able to demonstrate to the court that the petition debt has not been paid or secured or compounded (paragraph 12.5.1 of the PDIP). In cases where the petition is opposed, the fact that the debt hasn't been paid will be obvious; nonetheless, it is still a requirement for the petitioning creditor to still have a certificate of continuing debt. The certificate of continuing debt

[206] Darbyshire v Turpin [2013] EWHC 954 (Ch); [2013] B.P.I.R. 558 and Siddiqi v Taparis Ltd [2019] EWHC 417 (Ch); [2019] B.P.I.R. 1025. In Siddiqi, the appellate court overturned a first instance decision which, in view of the lateness of a Notice of Opposition, had treated a petition as unopposed.

is also very much necessary if the debtor fails to attend, and remains necessary on any adjourned hearing.

The PDIP contains some standard wording that can be used for the certificates, and some courts have pre-printed certificates which the petitioning creditor's lawyer or advocate can simply sign.

It sometimes occurs that the petitioning creditor does not attend the hearing. If, as a result, the petition is dismissed (this is the likely outcome unless another creditor is substituted, as to which, see the next paragraph), then by r. 10.26, the same petitioning creditor cannot, whether alone or jointly, present another petition against the same debtor in respect of the same debt without the permission of the court. A creditor seeking permission bears the burden of proof; the court will take into account whether a new petition would be an abuse of process, and also the adverse effects on a debtor of having to face a new petition.[207] If, in breach of r. 10.26, a petitioner presents a second petition, that petition can be cured as a technical defect under r. 12.64,[208] in other words retrospective permission is possible.

In a situation where the petitioning creditor does appear on the petition, but is found by the court not to be entitled to present a petition, or consents to withdraw the petition (or to the dismissal of the petition), or consents to an adjournment, or does not seek an order on the petition, then a person that has delivered notice under r. 10.19 can be substituted as petitioning creditor. The IR contain detailed provisions addressing the content of the substitution order: r. 10.28.

A like scenario is where a person who has given notice under r. 10.19 seeks an order for change of carriage of the petition under r. 10.29. The court will need to be satisfied that the original petitioning creditor

---

[207] Gordon v Omgate [2001] BPIR 909.

[208] Kasumu v Arrow Global (Guernsey) Ltd [2013] EWHC 789 (Ch), [2013] BPIR 1047.

intends to secure the postponement, adjournment, dismissal or withdrawal of the petition, or otherwise doesn't intend to prosecute it diligently.

If the court adjourns the hearing, it is the responsibility of the petitioning creditor to deliver notice of the order of adjournment to the debtor: r. 10.23(3).

If the court makes a bankruptcy order, the contents of the same are specified in r. 10.31. In almost every case, the court will (or should) take responsibility for production of the bankruptcy order.

Finally, if, for whatever reason, the petitioning creditor seeks an order dismissing the petition in advance of the hearing (or for permission to withdraw it), the petitioner must file a witness statement explaining the grounds or circumstances of the application if any person has given notice under r. 10.19 (or the court so orders). In practice, what tends to occur is that a payment is made by the debtor shortly before the hearing (or some other compromise is reached), so that the parties attend the hearing anyway: in that instance, because the hearing actually goes ahead, anybody who has given notice under r. 10.19 is not prejudiced. It is rare in those circumstances (where the hearing is going to go ahead anyway) for the petitioning creditor to serve a witness statement.

CHAPTER EIGHT

TECHNICAL POINTS

Introduction

There are several technical errors which can occur in respect of a petition. Limitations of space prevent us from discussing every possible scenario; instead, in this chapter we will set out the more common technical issues that can occur and the approach which the court takes to them.

(a) Contents of Petition

Generally, save for the matters explored in further detail below, errors in the contents of a petition will generally be capable of cure under r.12.64. Such errors are unlikely to have caused any prejudice to any party. However, a word of warning. This is ultimately a question of degree. A solitary error is unlikely to trouble the court; whereas a catalogue of errors can certainly lead to a court dismissing a petition under s.266(3).

Admittedly, that would be a particularly serious step for the court to take and it may be that the more proportionate order is that the petitioner amend the petition.

(b) Security?

Under r.10.9(1) the petition must state (subject to s.269) that the debt is unsecured. It can sometimes happen that a petition mistakenly suggests that the debt is unsecured (and in those circumstances fail to include the matters referred to in s.269).

A failure to disclose security is a serious procedural issue, however the court may grant leave for the petition to be amended and in considering whether to exercise its discretion in this regard, should "take account of at least the following factors: (i) the consequence of the breach (ii) the conduct of the parties and (iii) all the circumstances of the case."[209]

(c) Stale Petition?

Pursuant to r. 10.7(2):

"If the petition is based on a statutory demand, and more than four months have elapsed between the service of the demand and the presentation of the petition, the petition must explain the reasons for the delay."

In *Dunbar v Fowler*[210] the court highlighted that the purpose of such a rule was to prevent a party from relying upon a stale demand and that the question is whether the debtor has suffered any prejudice:

> "32. As far as I am aware there is no authority on this provision, and I have never heard argument on it before. Sealy and Milman's Annotated Guide to the Insolvency Legislation 2012 (15th Edition) says nothing about sub-rule (7). Muir Hunter on Personal Insolvency comments as follows:
>
> 7-267 This is presumably designed to give the court some control over the use of the bankruptcy process, and to prevent creditors relying on 'stale' statutory demands;

---

[209] State Bank of India v Mallya [2020] EWHC 1981 (Ch); [2021] B.P.I.R. 189 [20]; Barclays Bank Plc v Mogg [2003] EWHC 2645 (Ch); [2004] B.P.I.R. 259

[207] [2012] Lexis Citation 108

furthermore, Form 6.13A, at statutory note (f), itself requires a statement of 'reasons for the delay and explanations of the circumstances which have contributed to the late presentation of the petition.' In such cases, the debtor's financial position may have subsequently altered, and it might be unfair to allow a petition to be presented against him; alternatively, there may have been lengthy negotiations for payment or compromise of the debt between the creditor and the debtor, and the creditor may wish not simply to obtain a bankruptcy order, but to put further pressure on the debtor to pay or compromise the debt.

If the purpose of rule 6.12(7) is, as the learned authors of Muir Hunter contend, to prevent a petitioner from relying on a stale statutory demand (and I can think of no other purpose) it cannot be said to be a mischief requiring dismissal of the petition in the particular circumstances of this case. As we have seen, the statutory demand was served on 4 July 2011 (alternatively 4 August 2011 (see paragraph 6 of Mr Fowler's skeleton argument)) and the petition was presented on 26 March 2012, so the gap was just under eight months, almost double the time mentioned in sub-rule (7). It cannot be said that Mr Fowler has suffered any prejudice as a result of the further delay as a result of the passage of a further four months or thereabouts: he does not say he has suffered any prejudice, and plainly much of the time was taken up by the settlement negotiations to which I have referred, so Mr Fowler must have contemplated the possibility of a petition being presented throughout the whole of the period between service of the demand and presentation of petition, including the "extra" four months. The statutory demand cannot be said to be "stale" in the sense that Mr Fowler was lulled into any false sense of security about his position as a result of the delay in presenting the petition."

(d) Service of Petition

The position is the same as service of a statutory demand; a fundamental failure to serve a petition is incapable of cure under r.12.64.[211] Whereas, a petition which has actually reached an individual "or at least came within the dominion of, the intended recipient"[212] is capable of being cured under r.12.64.

In practice and as above, the court will typically seek to address any prejudice by granting an adjournment to ensure a debtor has sufficient time to deal with a petition. Whilst it is of course possible for a petition to be dismissed, in the authors experience, it is rare for the court to take that step.

---

211 Canning v Irwin Mitchell LLP [2017] EWHC 718 (Ch), [2017] BPIR 934; Gate Gourmet Luxembourg IV SARL v Morby [2016] EWHC 74 (Ch); [2016] B.P.I.R. 414 [55]

212 Canning v Irwin Mitchell LLP [2017] EWHC 718 (Ch), [2017] BPIR 934

CHAPTER NINE

COSTS

As always, costs are a matter of great importance. The key issues concern the costs position where:

- a bankruptcy order is made;
- a party successfully resists the making of a bankruptcy order, which can include circumstances where the petition debt is paid;
- multiple petitions.

Application of the CPR

Pursuant to r.12.1 IR, the provisions of the CPR concerning costs will apply.

Bankruptcy Order Made

Where a bankruptcy order is made, the costs of the petitioner and of any person appearing on the petition whose cost are allowed by the court are payable as an expense of the bankruptcy, pursuant to rule 10.149(i) IR.

The successful petitioner should simply seek an order that costs be payable as an expense of the bankruptcy.

It follows that no costs statement is required – it is usually better for an officeholder to assess the costs as opposed to the court as the former is likely to be more generous.[213]

No Bankruptcy Order Made

As always, there are some nuances to this. In the straightforward case of a party who successfully resists the making of a bankruptcy order, they will usually be entitled to payment of their costs. As already stated, it is an abuse of process to present a petition based on a genuinely disputed debt which can mean that the unsuccessful petitioner is vulnerable to an order for indemnity costs.

In the context of payment of the petition debt following service of the petition, in *Re Nowmost Company Limited*[214] (which also applies in the bankruptcy context[215]) it was held that:

- Where the petition debt is paid the usual practice is for the petitioner to be paid its costs.
- The onus is on the debtor to place before the court material which it sought to rely upon to displace the usual order for costs in the petitioner's favour. That material does not need to be formal evidence and it is for the judge to determine whether the usual practice should be displaced.

---

[213] By r. 12.42(1) IR, where the costs of any person are payable as an expense out of the insolvent estate, the amount payable must be decided by detailed assessment unless agreed between the office-holder and the person entitled to payment. In practice, it is extremely rare for an office-holder to require a detailed assessment to take place.

[214] [1997] BCC 105 at 108-109

[215] Oben v Blackman [2000] BPIR 302; [1999] B.C.C. 446 at 447.

So, in practice, the usual order following payment of the petition debt will be that the petitioner is entitled to its costs. It is of course possible for the debtor to displace the usual practice, but, in practice, those circumstances will not commonly occur.

Where a petition is defective and has led to an adjournment (to amend the petition perhaps) the debtor will normally be entitled to their costs.[216]

In *Grosvenor Estates Belgravia v Laidley*[217] the court clarified the costs position in circumstances where the petition debt is paid before service of the petition or where the petition is served after payment of any undisputed aspect of the petition debt is paid:

> *"[3] Where the debt, or the undisputed part, is paid before the petition has been served, the usual order is 'permission to withdraw the petition', unless the petition is served after payment, when the usual order is 'petition dismissed, no order as to costs'. In the first case no order for costs can be made, because, as the petition has not been served, there is no suit between the parties. In the second case an order for costs could be made, but it is not the practice of the court to penalise a debtor in costs, where he has paid the debt or undisputed part before there was a suit between the parties."*

Multiple Petitions

The Practice Direction – Insolvency Proceedings (the PDIP) specifically requires a petitioning creditor to carry out a search for whether a bankruptcy petition has already been presented against the debtor and

[216] [2000] BPIR 302; [1999] B.C.C. 446 447.

[217] [2010] BPIR 1090 at [3]

highlights the costs risk of proceeding when there is a prior petition pending:

> "**12.3.1** The petitioning creditor shall, before presenting a petition, conduct an Official Search with the Chief Land Registrar in the register of pending actions for pending petitions presented against the debtor and shall include the following certificate at the end of the petition:
>
> "I/we certify that within 7 days ending today, I/we have conducted a search for pending petitions presented against the debtor and that to the best of my/our knowledge, information, and belief [no prior petitions have been presented which are still pending] [a prior petition (No [ ]) has been presented and is/may be pending in the [Court] and I/we am/are issuing this petition at risk as to costs].Signed.....Dated....".

As is evident, whilst there is no prohibition against presenting a second petition the usual course to adopt is to simply appear as a supporting creditor on the first petition. An individual may nonetheless wish to proceed if it considers that neither change of carriage nor substitution are viable options.

In *In The Matter Of Glenn Maud Sub Nom (1) Edgeworth Capital (Luxembourg) Sarl (2) Libyan Investment Authority V Glenn Maud*[218] Snowden J (as he then was) held that:

> *"100. The natural reading of Rule 10.149(i) is that the costs of the petitioner and of any other person appearing on the petition which are given priority as expenses of the bankruptcy are those costs which relate to the petition upon which the bankruptcy order is made. Given the overall structure of the legislation, there*

[218] [2020] EWHC 1469 (Ch); [2020] B.P.I.R. 903.

> *is no obvious reason to read the rules more widely so as to enable the court to give priority in a bankruptcy to the costs of a petitioner in relation to a second petition upon which no order has been made."*

Albeit, in that case, the court allowed the costs of pursuing and supporting the petition upon which no order was made but on the basis as an unsecured claim in the bankruptcy rather than an expense.

Accordingly:

- If a prior petition is pending and a petitioner proceeds with their own petition, the first petition in time will be heard first.[219] The second petitioner should appear as a supporting creditor on that petition to obtain its costs of supporting it if a bankruptcy order is made. It may be at that hearing that the court is prepared to order that the second petitioner's costs of the second petition shall be recoverable as an unsecured claim in the bankruptcy.

- If a bankruptcy order is made on the first petition by the time the second petition comes on for hearing or before it comes on for hearing, the second petition will be dismissed and that petitioner will not receive its costs- in this way the risk identified in the PDIP will have been realised.

---

[219] [2019] EWHC 307 (Ch); [2019] B.P.I.R. 641 [39]

MORE BOOKS BY LAW BRIEF PUBLISHING

A selection of our other titles available now:-

- 'A Practical Guide to Probation Breaches and Other Applications' by Mark Thomas
- 'A Practical Guide to Remarriage and Divorce' by Cordelia Williams & Claire Howard
- 'A Practical Guide to Privacy, Transparency, Reporting Restrictions and Closed Proceedings in the Court of Protection' by Laura Mannering
- 'Beaumont on Barristers – A Guide to Defending Disciplinary Proceedings (Second Edition)' by Marc Beaumont
- 'A Practical Guide to Payments for Environmental Services' by Ben Sharples
- 'A Practical Guide to the Law of Pregnancy and Maternity at Work' by Rebecca Thomas
- 'A Practical Guide to Redundancy – Second Edition' by Philip Hyland & Collette Moore
- 'A Practical Guide to International Issues for Scottish Family Lawyers' by Susie Mountain, Donna McKay, Ken MacDonald
- 'A Practical Guide to the Law on Deprivation of Liberty' by Ben Troke
- 'A Practical Guide to Rights over Airspace and Subsoil – Second Edition' by Daniel Gatty
- 'A Practical Guide to the Law in Relation to Inquests' by Ramya Nagesh
- 'A Practical Guide to the Construction and Rectification of Wills and Trust Instruments (Second Edition)' by Edward Hewitt
- 'A Practical Guide to Data Protection in Social Housing' by Clare Paterson
- 'A Practical Guide to Spousal Maintenance – Second Edition' by Liz Cowell
- 'A Practical Guide to International Parental Child Abduction Law (England and Wales)' by Dr Onyója Momoh
- 'A Practical Guide to Deprivation of British Citizenship' by Sean Ell
- 'A Practical Guide to Commercial Property Service Charges' by Rachel Garton
- 'A Practical Guide to Clinical Negligence – Third Edition' by Geoffrey Simpson-Scott (Geoff)
- 'A Practical Guide to the Rights of Grandparents in Children Proceedings – Second Edition' by Stuart Barlow

'The Electronic Communications Code: A Practical Guide – Second Edition' by Kerry Bretherton KC, James Castle, Mark Loveday
'A Practical Guide to the Independent School Standards – September 2023 Edition' by Sarah McKimm
'A Practical Guide to Estate Administration and Crypto Assets' by Richard Marshall
'A Practical Guide to Parental Alienation in Private and Public Law Children Cases' by Sam King QC & Frankie Shama
'Contested Heritage – Removing Art from Land and Historic Buildings' by Richard Harwood QC, Catherine Dobson, David Sawtell
'The Limits of Separate Legal Personality: When Those Running a Company Can Be Held Personally Liable for Losses Caused to Third Parties Outside of the Company' by Dr Mike Wilkinson
'A Practical Guide to Transgender Law' by Robin Moira White & Nicola Newbegin
'A Practical Guide to 'Stranded Spouses' in Family Law' by Mani Singh Basi
'A Practical Guide to Residential Freehold Conveyancing' by Lorraine Richardson
'A Practical Guide to Pensions on Divorce for Lawyers' by Bryan Scant
'A Practical Guide to Challenging Sham Marriage Allegations in Immigration Law' by Priya Solanki
'A Practical Guide to Digital Communications Evidence in Criminal Law' by Sam Willis
'A Practical Guide to Legal Rights in Scotland' by Sarah-Jane Macdonald
'A Practical Guide to New Build Conveyancing' by Paul Sams & Rebecca East
'A Practical Guide to Inherited Wealth on Divorce' by Hayley Trim
'A Practical Guide to Practice Direction 12J and Domestic Abuse in Private Law Children Proceedings' by Rebecca Cross & Malvika Jaganmohan
'A Practical Guide to Confiscation and Restraint' by Narita Bahra QC, John Carl Townsend, David Winch
'A Practical Guide to the Law of Forests in Scotland' by Philip Buchan
'A Practical Guide to Health and Medical Cases in Immigration Law' by Rebecca Chapman & Miranda Butler
'A Practical Guide to Bad Character Evidence for Criminal Practitioners by Aparna Rao
'A Practical Guide to Extradition Law post-Brexit' by Myles Grandison et al
'A Practical Guide to Hoarding and Mental Health for Housing Lawyers' by Rachel Coyle

'Stephens on Contractual Indemnities' by Richard Stephens
'A Practical Guide to the EU Succession Regulation' by Richard Frimston
'A Practical Guide to Solicitor and Client Costs – Second Edition' by Robin Dunne
'Constructive Dismissal – Practice Pointers and Principles' by Benjimin Burgher
'A Practical Guide to Religion and Belief Discrimination Claims in the Workplace' by Kashif Ali
'A Practical Guide to the Law of Medical Treatment Decisions' by Ben Troke
'Fundamental Dishonesty and QOCS in Personal Injury Proceedings: Law and Practice' by Jake Rowley
'A Practical Guide to the Law in Relation to School Exclusions' by Charlotte Hadfield & Alice de Coverley
'A Practical Guide to Divorce for the Silver Separators' by Karin Walker
'The Right to be Forgotten – The Law and Practical Issues' by Melissa Stock
'A Practical Guide to Planning Law and Rights of Way in National Parks, the Broads and AONBs' by James Maurici QC, James Neill et al
'A Practical Guide to Election Law' by Tom Tabori
'A Practical Guide to the Law in Relation to Surrogacy' by Andrew Powell
'A Practical Guide to Claims Arising from Fatal Accidents – Second Edition' by James Patience
'A Practical Guide to Asbestos Claims' by Jonathan Owen & Gareth McAloon
'A Practical Guide to Stamp Duty Land Tax in England and Northern Ireland' by Suzanne O'Hara
'A Practical Guide to the Law of Farming Partnerships' by Philip Whitcomb
'A Practical Guide to the Law of Unlawful Eviction and Harassment – Second Edition' by Stephanie Lovegrove
'A Practical Guide to Costs in Personal Injury Claims – Second Edition' by Matthew Hoe
'A Practical Guide to the General Data Protection Regulation (GDPR) – Second Edition' by Keith Markham
'A Practical Guide to Working with Litigants in Person and McKenzie Friends in Family Cases' by Stuart Barlow
'Protecting Unregistered Brands: A Practical Guide to the Law of Passing Off' by Lorna Brazell
'A Practical Guide to Secondary Liability and Joint Enterprise Post-Jogee' by Joanne Cecil & James Mehigan

'A Practical Guide to the Pre-Action RTA Claims Protocol for Personal Injury Lawyers' by Antonia Ford

'A Practical Guide to Neighbour Disputes and the Law' by Alexander Walsh

'A Practical Guide to Coercive Control for Legal Practitioners and Victims' by Rachel Horman

'A Practical Guide to the Law of Driverless Cars – Second Edition'

by Alex Glassbrook, Emma Northey & Scarlett Milligan

'A Practical Guide to TOLATA Claims' by Greg Williams

'A Practical Guide to Elderly Law – Second Edition' by Justin Patten

'A Practical Guide to Responding to Housing Disrepair and Unfitness Claims' by Iain Wightwick

'A Practical Guide to the Law of Bullying and Harassment in the Workplace' by Philip Hyland

'How to Be a Freelance Solicitor: A Practical Guide to the SRA-Regulated Freelance Solicitor Model' by Paul Bennett

'A Practical Guide to Prison Injury Claims' by Malcolm Johnson

'A Practical Guide to Advising Clients at the Police Station' by Colin Stephen McKeown-Beaumont

'A Practical Guide to Antisocial Behaviour Injunctions – Second Edition' by Iain Wightwick

'Practical Mediation: A Guide for Mediators, Advocates, Advisers, Lawyers, and Students in Civil, Commercial, Business, Property, Workplace, and Employment Cases' by Jonathan Dingle with John Sephton

'The Mini-Pupillage Workbook' by David Boyle

'A Practical Guide to Crofting Law' by Brian Inkster

'A Practical Guide to the Law of Domain Names and Cybersquatting' by Andrew Clemson

'A Practical Guide to the Law of Gender Pay Gap Reporting' by Harini Iyengar

'NHS Whistleblowing and the Law' by Joseph England

'Employment Law and the Gig Economy' by Nigel Mackay & Annie Powell

'A Practical Guide to Noise Induced Hearing Loss (NIHL) Claims' by Andrew Mckie, Ian Skeate, Gareth McAloon

'An Introduction to Beauty Negligence Claims – A Practical Guide for the Personal Injury Practitioner' by Greg Almond

'Intercompany Agreements for Transfer Pricing Compliance' by Paul Sutton

'Zen and the Art of Mediation' by Martin Plowman

'A Practical Guide to Adoption for Family Lawyers' by Graham Pegg

'A Practical Guide to Industrial Disease Claims' by Andrew Mckie & Ian Skeate
'A Practical Guide to Conducting a Sheriff Court Proof' by Andrew Stevenson
'A Practical Guide to Vicarious Liability' by Mariel Irvine
'A Practical Guide to Applications for Landlord's Consent and Variation of Leases' by Mark Shelton
'A Practical Guide to Relief from Sanctions Post-Mitchell and Denton' by Peter Causton
'A Practical Guide to Equity Release for Advisors' by Paul Sams
'A Practical Guide to Financial Services Claims' by Chris Hegarty
'A Practical Guide to Financial Ombudsman Service Claims' by Adam Temple & Robert Scrivenor
'A Practical Guide to Running Housing Disrepair and Cavity Wall Claims – Second Edition' by Andrew Mckie & Ian Skeate
'A Practical Guide to Holiday Sickness Claims – Second Edition' by Andrew Mckie & Ian Skeate
'Arguments and Tactics for Personal Injury and Clinical Negligence Claims' by Dorian Williams
'A Practical Guide to Drone Law' by Rufus Ballaster, Andrew Firman, Eleanor Clot
'On Experts: CPR35 for Lawyers and Experts' by David Boyle
'An Introduction to Personal Injury Law' by David Boyle

www.ingramcontent.com/pod-product-compliance
Lightning Source LLC
LaVergne TN
LVHW022101200926
848481LV00003B/1026
9781918241174